W9-AAT-460

Top Ten in Advertising

I LOVE YOU, TOO.
BMW
MPH
km/h
1/min
x1000
MPG
I/0

TopTenInAdvertising

CEO & Creative Director: B. Martin Pedersen

Publisher: Doug Wolske
Publications Director: Michael Gerbino

Editor: Andrea Birnbaum

Art Director: Lauren Slutsky
Design & Production Assistant: Joseph Liotta

Published by Graphis Inc.

Dedicated to the memory of Helmut Krone
1925–1996

BMW shares its passion for driving—and for its customers—in this 1993 Fallon ad; photo by Mark LaFavor (see page 56)

Contents

 For more information on Graphis books, visit our Web site at www.graphis.com. ISBN:1-888001-95-X Printed in Hong Kong by DNP.

This Diet Guarana Antarctica ad brought worldwide attention to DM9, and is still a symbol of simplicity and representative imagery; photo by Cassio Vasconcellos *(see page 30)*

Over the past decade, the editors at Graphis have had numerous occasions to view the work of hundreds of advertising agencies from around the world. This includes submissions to the Graphis Advertising Annual (published each year for nearly two decades) and the bimonthly magazine, Graphis.

In the course of selecting and editing these publications, we have been struck by the consistency, artistry and inventiveness of an elite group of agencies. These agencies are clearly driven by quality creative work, which has resulted in producing some of the most astounding and memorable ads. These campaigns have etched their client's brand in the customer's mind. Presented in this book are ten of these agencies, whom Graphis has chosen as the best in the business. Simply put: these are some of the most successful ad agencies in the world at getting a client's message out.

Please note that while Graphis has selected the work presented here, we asked each of the agencies to make a statement about themselves, in their own words, to serve as an introduction to their portfolio. Graphis extends our thanks and congratulations to the staff and principals of each of the agencies for their assistance and cooperation in compiling this volume. Also to their clients, who have had the good taste, earned trust and courage to partner with such magnificent talent. The agencies represent the notion that, in the words of Helmut Krone, to whom this book is dedicated, "it's the idea that counts."

This photo never appeared in The New Yorker, *but, paired with excerpted text, this Goodby, Silverstein & Partners campaign made quite a splash; photo by Dan Escobar* *(see page 68)*

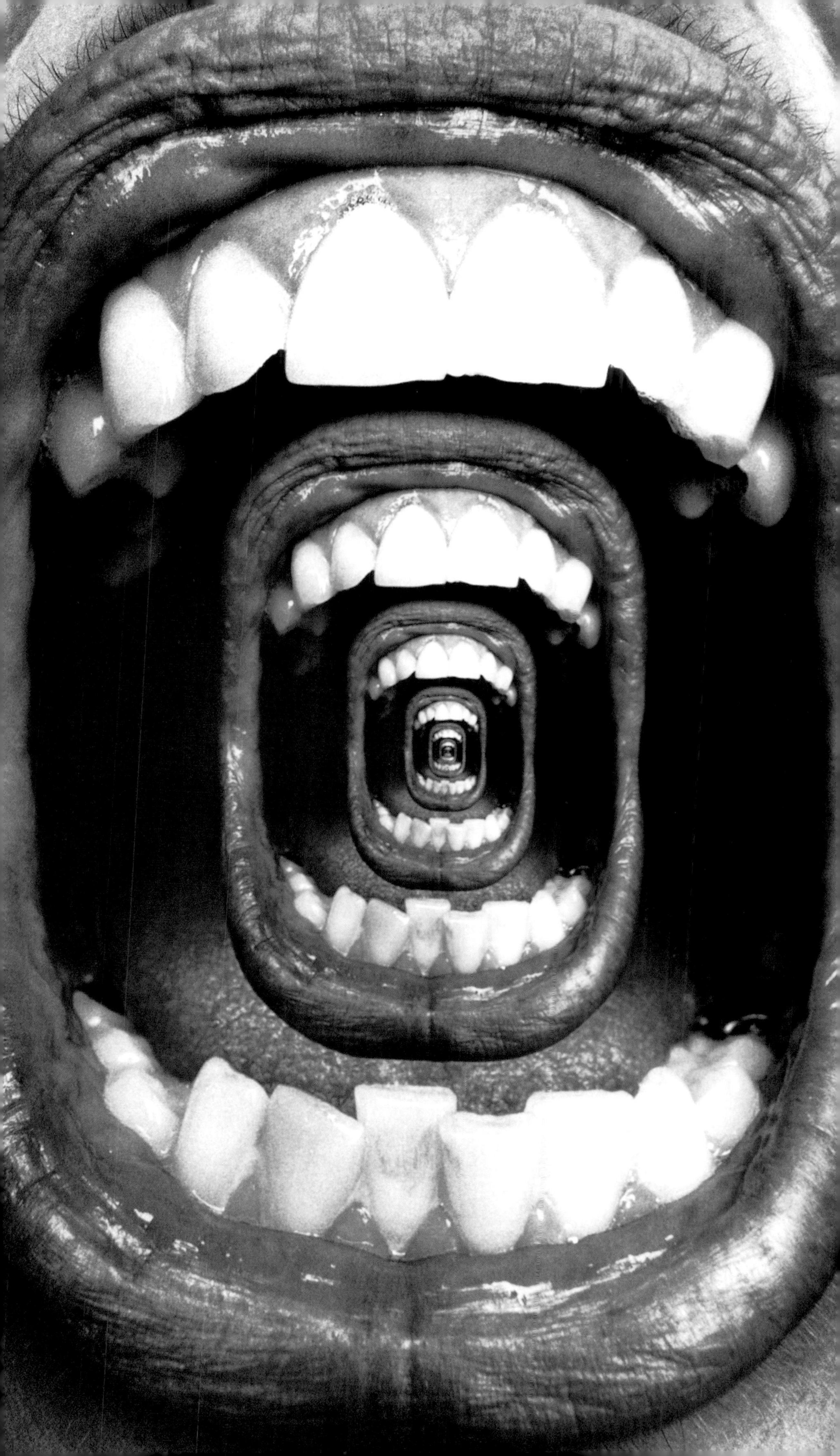

Foreword By Warren Berger

"When advertising is artfully made, people don't want to bypass it; they actually want to savor it."

We've reached an interesting period in advertising: Almost everyone agrees that this form of communication is on the cusp of enormous change, but no one is certain what forms the change will take. There are plenty of people willing to make blind predictions, and eager to sound warning bells. ■ We're told the 30-second commercial will soon be history, thanks to the convergence of computer and television, the rise of interactive technology, and the availability of digital video recorder/TV gadgets like *TiVo*. The basic thinking is that as technology provides people with more choices, they will choose to bypass commercials. And what of print ads? The doomsayers don't even bother to predict the demise of print; they assume it's already dead. After all, how can a static image on a page possibly compete with an interactive website? By extension, this is also taken to mean that advertising agencies (except for newcomers with a dot-com on their name) are an endangered species, poor dinosaurs relying on old methods in a new world. ■ I wonder: Have any of the people who say such things ever seen the TV commercials of the San Francisco agency Goodby, Silverstein & Partners? Have they ever gone to South America and been stopped in their tracks by a billboard from São Paulo's DM9 agency? Or flipped through a magazine and discovered the best things in it were the print ads by Fallon of Minneapolis? If they had, they would know two things: 1) When advertising is artfully made, people don't want to bypass it; they actually want to savor it. And, 2) Nothing that has appeared on the Internet so far has anywhere near the power of the old-media work of these agencies. ■ Not to say it won't happen, eventually. As advertising morphs into new shapes and forms, it may very well end up being as compelling as a Harley Davidson print ad from Carmichael Lynch. And when that does happen, don't be surprised if these 10 agencies are leading the way. Ogilvy & Mather, in fact, has already made a good start in new media, by seamlessly tying together its online and offline ad campaigns for clients like IBM. ■ But for the present, and perhaps for some time to come, the most interesting and persuasive pieces of communication are coming to us via television and print. And they're being generated by the 10 agencies in this book. These agencies are not all alike. Go down the list and you'll find big agencies and small ones. Some operate out of large office towers; on the other hand, Amsterdam's KesselsKramer is humbly quartered in a 19th-century church. These agencies are based in bustling cities like New York and São Paulo, as well as quieter towns, like Charlotte, North Carolina. Some are in places not generally thought of as advertising hotbeds—who would've expected a South African agency, or one from New Zealand, to rank among the world's top 10? ■ They do, however, have a couple of things in common. One is an awareness that advertising is a delicate balance of art and science, of entertainment and strategy. If you look closely, you'll see that this is a common thread running through all of the work on display in this book. The styles of the ads vary greatly-from classic design to contemporary, from outrageous humor to logical appeals. But all of these ads do the two things great advertising must do: They engage you (the art/entertainment half of the equation) and they make the product or brand relevant to you (the science/strategy part of the equation). Most advertisers are simply unable to achieve and maintain this balance, and fall toward one side or the other; they sell too hard in the ads, or they don't sell enough. Only the best agencies manage to walk that tightrope. ■ Something else these agencies share is an understanding that good advertising begins with smart and original ideas, and ends with painstaking execution and attention to detail. There are no shortcuts; you can't rely on the magic of photography, or computer-aided design, or film special effects. All of that may help along the way, but only if the work is fundamentally grounded in solid, original thinking. At all of these agencies, the idea is king. This is worth emphasizing to those futurists who think interactivity, rich media and other technological improvements will radically alter the fundamentals of good communication in days ahead. Don't bet on it. It's safe to predict that in any medium, good communication will always be about great ideas, elegantly expressed. And as long at that's the case, the Top Ten agencies in this book will remain at the leading edge of advertising.

Warren Berger is the founding editor of One, *a magazine about advertising. He's also a contributing editor at* Wired *and* Advertising Age, *and is a frequent contributor to* The New York Times. *His book,* Advertising Today, *is about modern advertising.*

Saatchi & Saatchi illustrates the cyclical nature of verbal abuse in this powerful ad for New Zealand Children & Young Persons Service; digital image by Andy Salisbury (page 148) Following page: Carmichael Lynch reinvents the Gibson image (page 16)

Carmichael Lynch

O'DONOVAN'S

The moment you pass through the doors of Carmichael Lynch, you know: this is anything but advertising as usual. There is something deeper at work here. It springs from our leadership. It's embodied in our culture. The people here are real. Funny. Loyal. Hardworking. Intelligent. Irrepressible. Fiercely committed to furthering one simple philosophy: an unwavering belief in the power of an idea. ■ Make it simple. Make it resonate. Make people not just see an ad, but feel it. Listen to our clients. Challenge our clients. Work together to seize the highest ground. And build brands that unflinchingly withstand all challenges. ■ Throughout CL's 39-year history, we've watched our client roster evolve into one of the most enviable in the world. With each client, and each new client, we keep learning and evolving creatively to take on new challenges—without ever forgetting that the strength is always in the idea. Life should be so simple.

pictured from left to right: Bill Hogan, Sheldon Clay, Ember Kapitan, Peter Huxmann, Glen Wachowiak, Jeff Terwilliger, Anne Carlson, Jennifer Buley, Jennifer David, Tom Holler, Shane Johnson, Blair Fellman, Rhonda Muller, Brian Kroening, Adam Demers, Kellie Johnson Kegley, Frank Haggerty, Kim Bryant, Tanya Ryan, Amy Olesen, Rebecca Gienz, Sandy Boss Febbo, Jack Steinmann, Randy Hughes, Steve Casey, Tom Witkowki, Eric Sorensen, Linda Hines, Dan Roettger, Kathy Umland, Hans Hansen, James Clunie, Bonnie Butler, Jack Supple, Christine Moe, Judy Savage, Joa Oberle, Choong Lee, Audery Cullen, Pam Cook, Laurie McElroy, Louia Thompson, Bob Berken, Jason Smith, Michael Atkinson, Randy Tatum, Gary Koelling, Scott Stoddard, Dan Joppa, Brynn Hausmann, Damon Bay, Brenda Clemons, Sean Healey, Jud Smith.

Client: OMC/Stratos **Creative and Art Director:** Brian Kroening **Copywriter:** Derek Pletch **Account Executive:** Jason White **Photographer:** Clint Clemens **Production:** Stacy Richards

Carmichael Lynch

How Far Would You Go
If *Nothing* Was Holding You Back?

A deck should never fence you in. Set yourself free with Trex® Easy Care Decking®. No sealing. No splinters. No limits. Visit *www.trex.com* or call 1-800-BUY-TREX ext.371 for a book of inspiration.

Trex
The DECK of a Lifetime.

Think *Outside* The Rectangle.

It's amazing what you can dream up when you're not busy sealing or staining. Trex® Easy Care Decking®. For a book full of inspiration, call 1-800-BUY-TREX ext. 300 or visit www.trex.com.

Trex®
The DECK of a Lifetime.™

Client: Trex Decking **Creative Director:** Jud Smith **Art Director:** Jeff Terwilliger **Copywriter:** Steve Casey **Account Executive:** Jaye Peterson **Photographers:** Shawn Michienzi/RipSaw **Production:** Brenda Clemons

Client: Gibson Guitar Corporation **Creative Director:** Brian Kroening **Art Director:** Randy Hughes **Copywriter:** Glen Wachowiak **Account Executives:** Gina Signorella, Ryan Skubic **Photographer:** Shawn Michienzi/Ripsaw **Production:** Tom Holler

Client: American Standard **Creative Director:** Brian Kroening **Art Director:** Randy Hughes **Copywriter:** Glen Wachowiak **Account Executives:** Sara Piepgras, Joe Summary **Photographer:** Steve Henke **Production:** Linda Hines

Revered in 142 countries.
Rapala
The Legendary Finnish Minnow.

Renko Dalliinen. Rapala eye painter since 1954.

Rapala
The Legendary Finnish Minnow.

Life before Rapalas.

Rapala
The Legendary Finnish Minnow.

May your doorknob always smell of fish.

Rapala
The Legendary Finnish Minnow.

Client: Normark Brand **Creative Director:** Jim Nelson **Art Director:** Frank Haggerty **Copywriter:** Jim Nelson **Account Executives:** Paula Perry, Dave Link, Mark Meadows **Photographers:** Shawn Michienze/RipSaw **Production:** Louia Thompson

Press the accelerator of the 911 Turbo, and what happens next is astonishing. The raw surge of power. The incredibly [illegible] balance. Yes, it's crazy to take automotive achievement to such an extreme. That may be the best reason of all. Contact us at 1-800-PORSCHE or porsche.com.

Keeps the logical side of the brain pinned to the back of your skull.

Instant freedom, courtesy of the Boxster S. The 250 horsepower boxer engine launches you forward with its distinctive growl. Any memory of life on a leash evaporates in the wind rushing overhead. It's time to run free. Contact us at 1-800-PORSCHE or porsche.com.

What a dog feels when the leash breaks.

The day you go from dreaming about the 911 Carrera Cabriolet to actually owning one is like nothing else. The timeless, flowing lines. The 300 horsepower boxer engine. No, sleep will not come. We suggest a top-down drive in the cool midnight air. Contact us at 1-800-PORSCHE or porsche.com.

Try going to sleep the first night you have this in your garage.

Client: Porsche **Creative Director:** Jud Smith **Art Directors:** Hans Hansen, Michael Hart **Copywriters:** Sheldon Clay, Michael Hart **Account Executives:** Mark Meadows, Shane Hipps, Craig Rowley **Photographer:** Georg Fischer **Production:** Brenda Clemons Carmichael Lynch

Client: Brown Forman/McPherson **Creative Director:** Jennifer Johnson **Art Director:** Dave Damman **Copywriter:** Michael Hart **Account Executive:** Tom Costello **Photographer:** Shawn Michienze/RipSaw **Production:** Brenda Clemons

TRADITION IS FINE FOR THOSE WHO WANT TO LOOK BACKWARD.

AVOID THE CURSE OF NOSTALGIA.

SOME ARE ATTACHED TO THE OLD WAYS LIKE A BALL IS ATTACHED TO A CHAIN.

Client: Volvo **Creative Director:** Jud Smith **Art Director:** Hans Hanson **Copywriter:** Glen Wachowiak **Account Executive:** Jim Scott **Photographer:** Darren Ross **Production:** Louis Thompson

Carmichael Lynch

Advertising

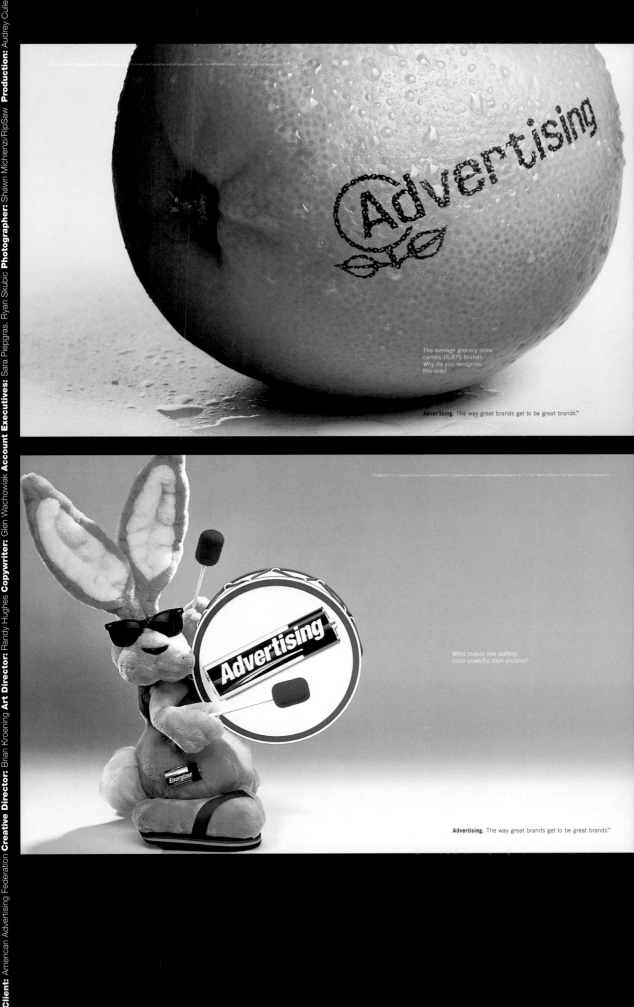

The average grocery store carries 16,875 brands. Why do you recognize this one?

Advertising. The way great brands get to be great brands.™

Advertising

Energizer

What makes one battery more powerful than another?

Advertising. The way great brands get to be great brands.™

Client: American Advertising Federation **Creative Director:** Brian Kroening **Art Director:** Randy Hughes **Copywriter:** Glen Wachowiak **Account Executives:** Sara Piepgras, Ryan Skubic **Photographer:** Shawn Michienzi/RipSaw **Production:** Audrey Culle

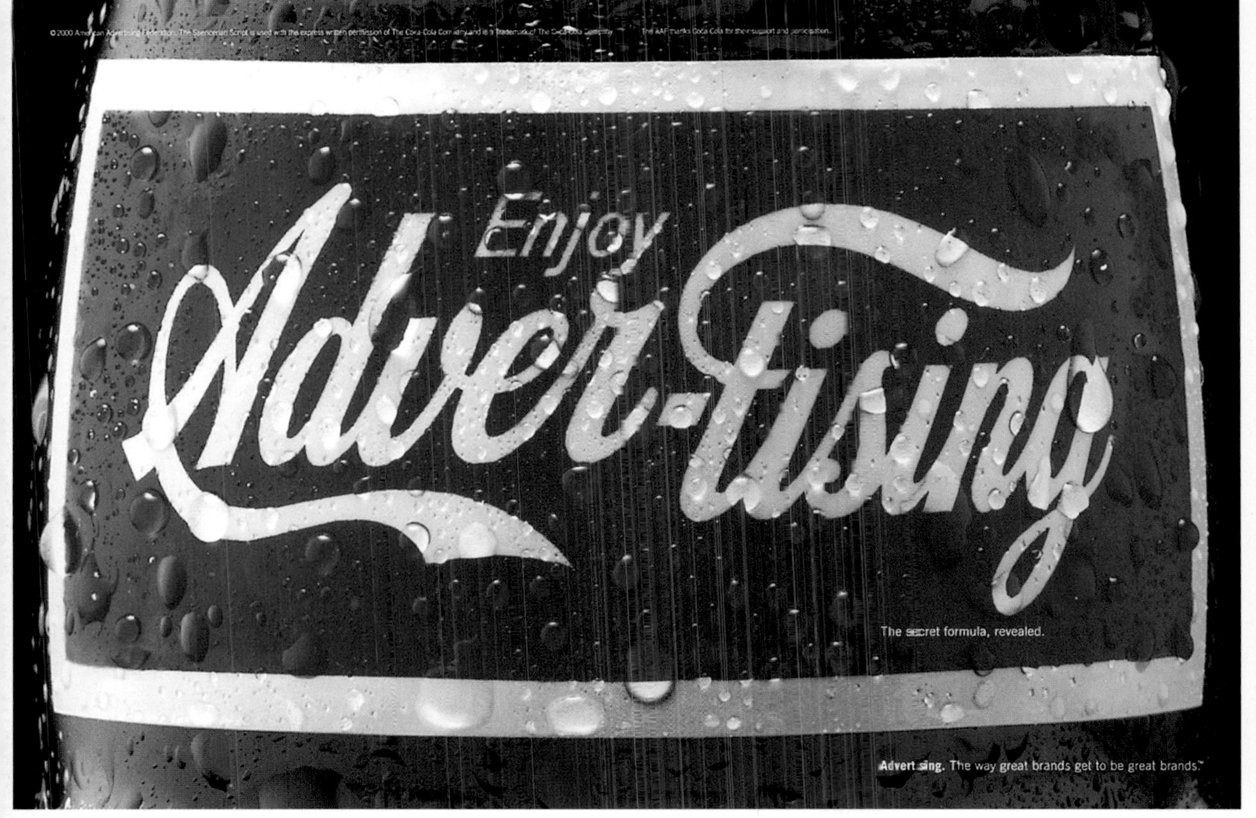
Enjoy
Adver-tising
The secret formula, revealed.
Advertising. The way great brands get to be great brands.

EARTH. AS VIEWED FROM HEAVEN.

Riding along a highway on a Harley-Davidson® motorcycle, relaxed and easy. If there's anything better than this, we haven't found it. Wheels spin. Chrome flashes. Fresh wind clears out your head. Thick Harley® sound pours out your pipes. And the world comes at you over the bars. Mountain ranges, waterfalls, redwood trees, one-horse towns, Civil War battlefields, armadillos, steel grate bridges, rusty farm

trucks, muddy rivers, gigantic skies, adventure: an infinity of things you can only experience by being on the road breathing them in. Generations of riders would tell you they could happily spend eternity here. If you think you could, too, call 1-800-443-2153 or visit www.harley-davidson.com for your nearest H-D dealer.

The Legend Rolls On.™

YOU COMMIT 4 OF THE 7 DEADLY SINS JUST LOOKING AT IT.

Behold the cutting edge of Harley-Davidson custom styling. Pure tradition, pushed to a place it's never been. To the trained eye it's brand new, yet instantly classic. Note the clean front end, stretched fuel tank and one-of-a-kind rear fender (Lust). Check the attention to detail evidenced in the braided steel hoses, small turn signals and recessed taillight (Envy). It all combines for a look that would

put many a custom show bike to shame (Pride). And at the center is a twin balanced, Twin Cam 88B™ engine: the biggest, smoothest, strongest motor to ever power a Softail® (Gluttony). The Softail Deuce.™ Nobody else does it like this. Welcome to temptation. Call us at 1-800-443-2153 or visit www.harley-davidson.com for your local dealer.

The Legend Rolls On.™

RIDE. BECAUSE CHILDREN NEED HEROES.

Think back. Maybe you can remember the first time you saw a rider on a Harley-Davidson® motorcycle. Maybe you were waiting for the bus or playing ball with some other kids. Suddenly there they were, steel and leather and a sound that traveled through your ears right down into the pit of your stomach. It was cowboys and indians and astronauts all rolled into one. Huge,

in living color, right in front of your eyes. When you're a kid, anything is possible and so you knew right then, that someday, you'd be the one commanding the big Harley.® Well, someday has come. Time to ride. Time to get free. Time to do for kids what that very first rider did for you. Call us at 1-800-443-2153 or visit www.harley-davidson.com for your nearest dealer.

The Legend Rolls On.™

Client: Harley-Davidson **Creative Director:** Jim Nelson **Art Director:** Hans Hansen **Copywriter:** Eric Sorensen **Account Executive:** Scott Baker **Photographers:** Madison Ford, Joe Paczkowski/Ripsaw **Production:** Brenda Clemons

Page 14 *OMC/Stratos* The objective was to get hardcore bass fisherman to consider Stratos in a highly cluttered bass boat market. With themes of looks, speed and success, we connected with the raw, emotional side of our audience.

Page 15 *Trex Decking* In their quest to become the definitive leader in composite decking materials, Trex has chosen to sell dreams rather than planks. This campaign is about aspiring to build the deck of one's dreams. The ads, which run in yard and garden magazines, depend on stunning "haven't seen that before" decks to whet the appetites of prospective buyers. Step two after seeing these ads is for the consumer to request more information. And the response has been as stunning as the images.

Page 16 *Gibson Guitars* In an industry where image is everything, Gibson's image had started to soften. The "Pure" campaign sets out to reclaim Gibson's rightful position as the biggest, baddest, most emulated guitar in the world.

Page 17 *American Standard* The goal was to introduce a brand new line of bathroom products designed in Europe and built to American plumbing specifications. Ads targeted architects and designers.

Page 18 *Normark Brand* In fishing circles, Rapala lures are regarded as the most finely crafted, best-designed, trusted fishing lures in the world. This campaign runs on the back cover of sporting magazines and was designed to reinforce that perception. Fun, simple reminders of the Rapala mystique strengthen the connection anglers have to the brand.

Page 19 *Porsche* Porsche Cars North America, while preparing to launch a Sports Utility Vehicle in 2002, has a communications objective of continuing to strengthen their brand's image, core values and perceptions. Rather than reposition the compnay, this campaign focuses on the very heart of what Porsche gives to their drivers, what only Porsche brings to driving. Like the cars, the design and photography of the ads strive to be simple and tasteful yet always powerful. The copy is confident and unflinching as it presents the brand experience.

Page 20 *Brown Forman/McPherson–Wines of Australia* This campaign set out to introduce McPherson wine as an alternative to California wines. The unique heritage and geography of Australia was used as the platform for the ideas. The message was perfect for this category where consumers are always interested in trying something new and different.

Page 21 *Volvo* Volvo Trucks North America provides progressive products, services and ideas that enhance the lives of transportation professionals. Unlike many competitors, Volvo has no desire to rest on tradition with an emphasis only on vehicles. Instead, Volvo considers innovation, service and new business ideas to be more important in today's market. This campaign supports and communicates Volvo's position as an industry leader. At the same time, it rallies around forward thinking and derides any desire to stick with tradition. Simple, elegant photography gives a contemporary look to support singular headlines that challenge convention. It's "New Roads," for Volvo.

Page 22-23 *American Advertising Federation* "The Power of Advertising" campaign set out to remind business executives that advertising is a key component to the success of their business, not a dispensable line item. To prove this we used shining examples of successful brands that have been consistent with their marketing effort over the years.

Page 24 *Harley-Davidson* Before we started work on this campaign, we got together with our client and put up the last ten years of Harley advertising to see if we could identify the characteristics of the most successful ads. The result: Bold statements built on simple Harley Davidson truths make the Harley Davidson ads that connect most powerfully with the people the brand needs to reach. We call them big, thundering Harley ads.

Page 25 *Harley-Davidson* The goal of this campaign is to separate Harley-Davidson Genuine Motor Accessories from a sea of after-market competitors offering custom accessories for Harley-Davidson motorcycles. These competitors run advertising that shows all the bits and pieces of chrome they offer, but doesn't give anyone any idea of how it all goes together. Our strategy is to show the "Dream Bikes" that are built from Harley accessories and offer the catalog as a sort of manual to help riders create one of their own. On top of that, we put words that make the brand likeable to the riders.

Carmicheal Lynch 800 Hennepin Avenue Minneapolis, Minnesota 55403 tel. 612-334-6000 fax. 612-334-6090

DM9DDB

Established on September 19, 1989, within 11 years DM9 DDB became the most awarded Brazilian advertising agency and the second largest agency in Brazil in billings. The president, Affonso Serra, was elected the Adman of the Year at Colunistas Brazil award 2000 and has been recently elected member of DDB Worldwide International Board. ■ Its joint venture with the multinational DDB in 1997 marked the greatest deal ever in the history of Brazilian advertising. DM9 DDB's ascension broke all records on the Brazilian advertising market, jumping from the 93rd position in late 1989 to second place in 1999. That is even more impressive when we consider the steadiness of its growth which, in addition to showing a low client turnover rate, has been greater than the growth of the Brazilian market in general. In 1999, its billings were R$ 404 million (17% more than in 1998). ■ Our partner DDB is the second largest US advertising agency network, third in the world and has 206 offices in 99 countries, serving more than 1300 clients. ■ Voted the most creative and efficient by the 60 largest advertisers in Brazil in a survey held in the end of 1999 by the financial newspaper Gazeta Mercantil, DM9 DDB is recognized, both nationally and internationally, not only for its creative brilliance, but also for its entrepreneurial performance. ■ DM9 DDB has clients such as AOL, Microsoft, Parmalat, Honda (Automobiles and Motorcycles), American Airlines, Clorox, Johnson & Johnson, Souza Cruz (B.A.T.) and Telefonica. ■ Chosen the best agency in the 1999 Cannes International Advertising Festival, repeating 1998´s success, DM9 DDB is the first agency not headquartered in New York or London to be chosen "Agency of the Year" by the most important worldwide Advertising Festival. ■ In nine years only, gathered 43 Lions and 1 Grand Prix, from Cannes Festival—including 2 Cyber Lions. It was the first agency in Brazil who got a Grand Prix at Cannes Festival besides winning two Grand Prix at The New York Festivals and FIAP (Iberian-American Advertising Festival) and one at Clio Awards. The best Iberian-American Agency 94-98—El Ojo de Iberoamerica. And won a Gold Pencil at One Show Interactive. ■ We've also got the Marketing Best Award as one of the Best Companies of the Century. And DM9 DDB was elected the 6th most creative New Media Agency in the world by the International Digital Excellence Association (IDEA). ■ DM9 DDB is recognized for putting together a bright creative team. The creative committee consists of two creative VPs: Erh Ray (who created, for instance, the Mammal campaign for Parmalat) and Sergio Valente (who participated in the presidential election campaign), besides the VPs, DM9 DDB has three creative directors: Camila Franco (who created one of the most famous Brazilian campaigns: "The first bra") and Jader Rossetto and Pedro Cappeletti (the most awarded creative duo of DM9 DDB with 15 Cannes Lions in just 6 years) DM9 DDB is now located on the two top floors of São Paulo's tallest building, with a 360° panoramic view of the city.

Creative Directors, pictured front to back, left to right: Erh Ray, Pedro Cappeletti, Camela Franco, Sergio Valente, Jader Rossetto, Ciro Silva; Creative Team pictured behind

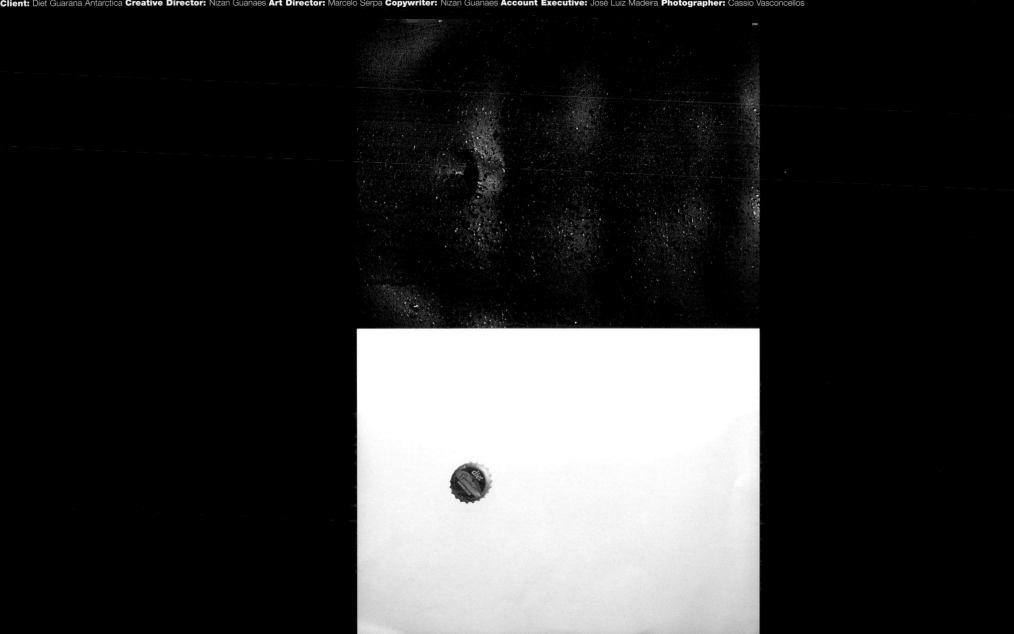

Client: Diet Guarana Antarctica **Creative Director:** Nizan Guanaes **Art Director:** Marcelo Serpa **Copywriter:** Nizan Guanaes **Account Executive:** José Luiz Madeira **Photographer:** Cassio Vasconcellos

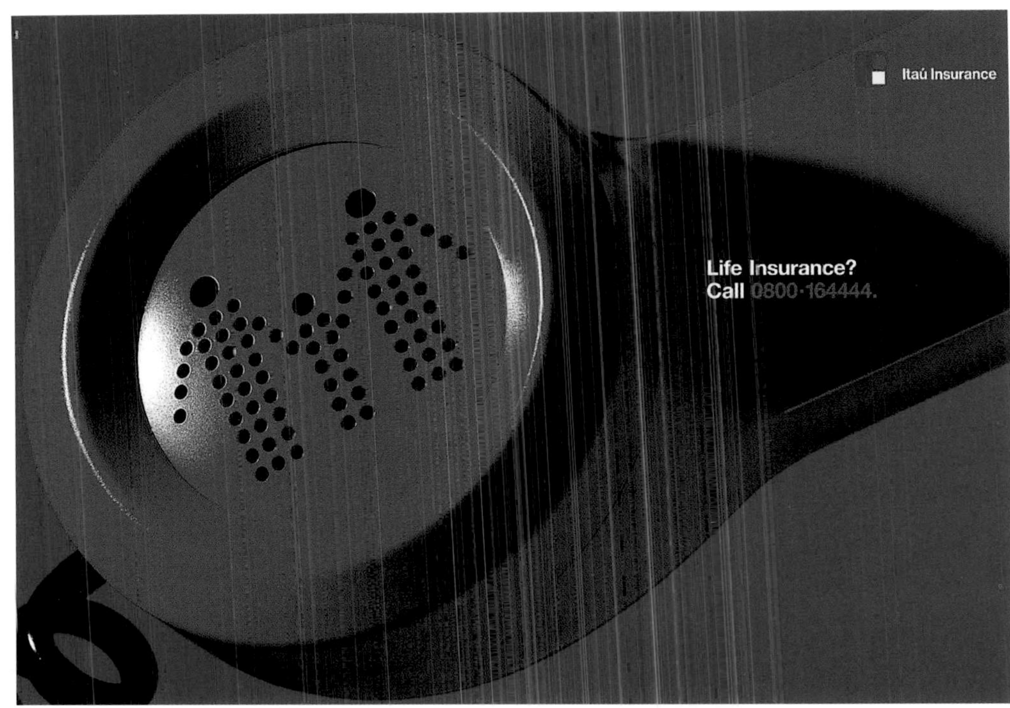

Client: Itau Insurance **Creative Directors:** Nizan Guanaes, Tomás Lorente **Art Directors:** Erh Ray, Tomás Lorente **Copywriter:** José Henrique Borghi **Account Executive:** Ana Paula Grassmann **Photographer:** Richard Kohout

REX

Parmalat Fortified Milk. It gives you more energy.

Parmalat
Fortified Milk.
It gives you
more energy.

Parmalat Fortified Milk. It helps you grow stronger.

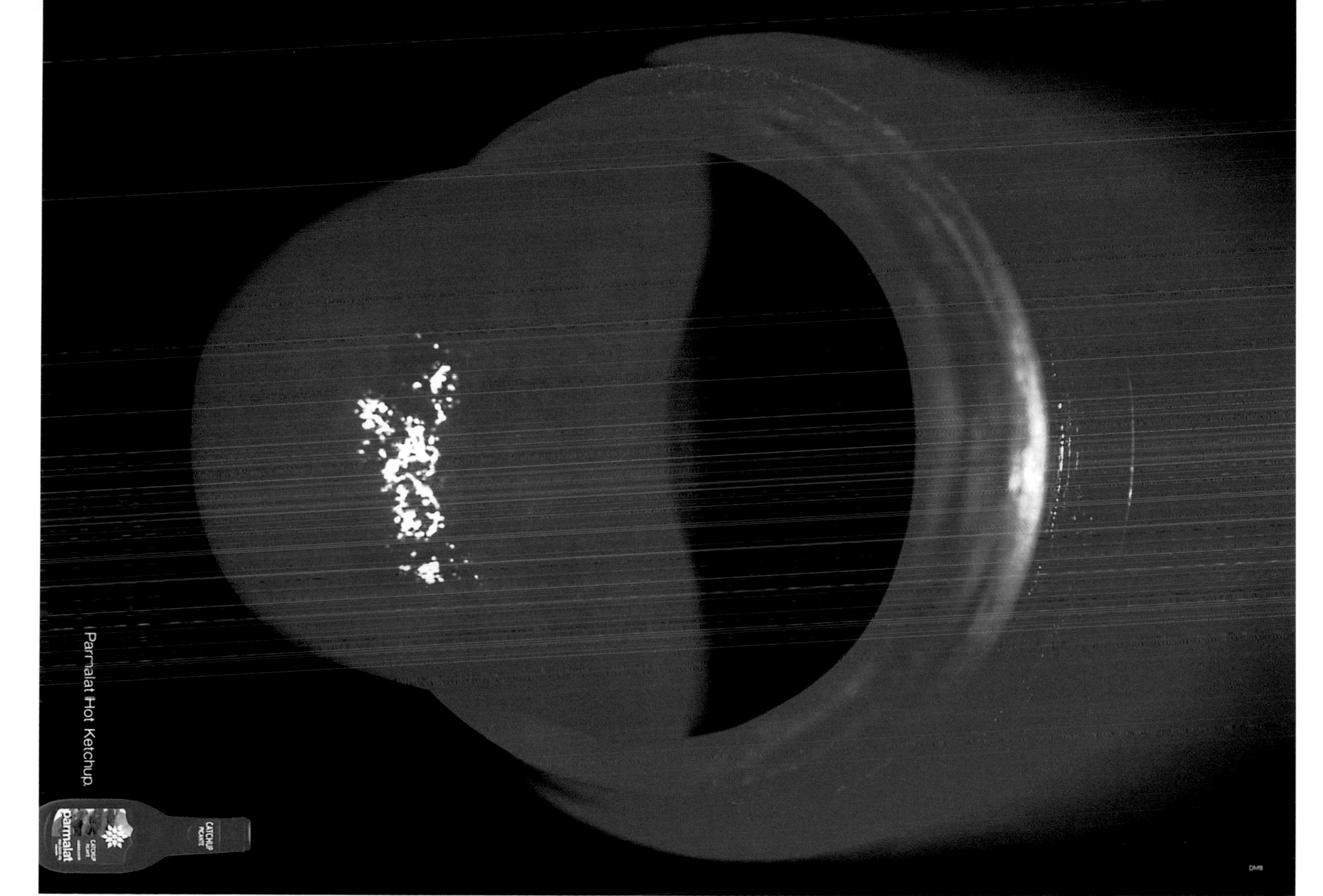

Client: Parmalat **Creative Directors:** Tomás Lorente, Carlos Domingos **Art Director:** Eugênio Duarte **Copywriter:** Alexandre Lucas **Account Executive:** Eduardo Linhares **Photographer:** Fabio Bataglia

Client: Honda **Creative Directors:** Nizan Guanaes, Tomás Lorente **Art Director:** Pedro Cappeletti **Copywriter:** Jáder Rossetto **Account Executive:** Ana Paula Grassmann **Photographer:** Ale Catan **Production:** Stacy Richards

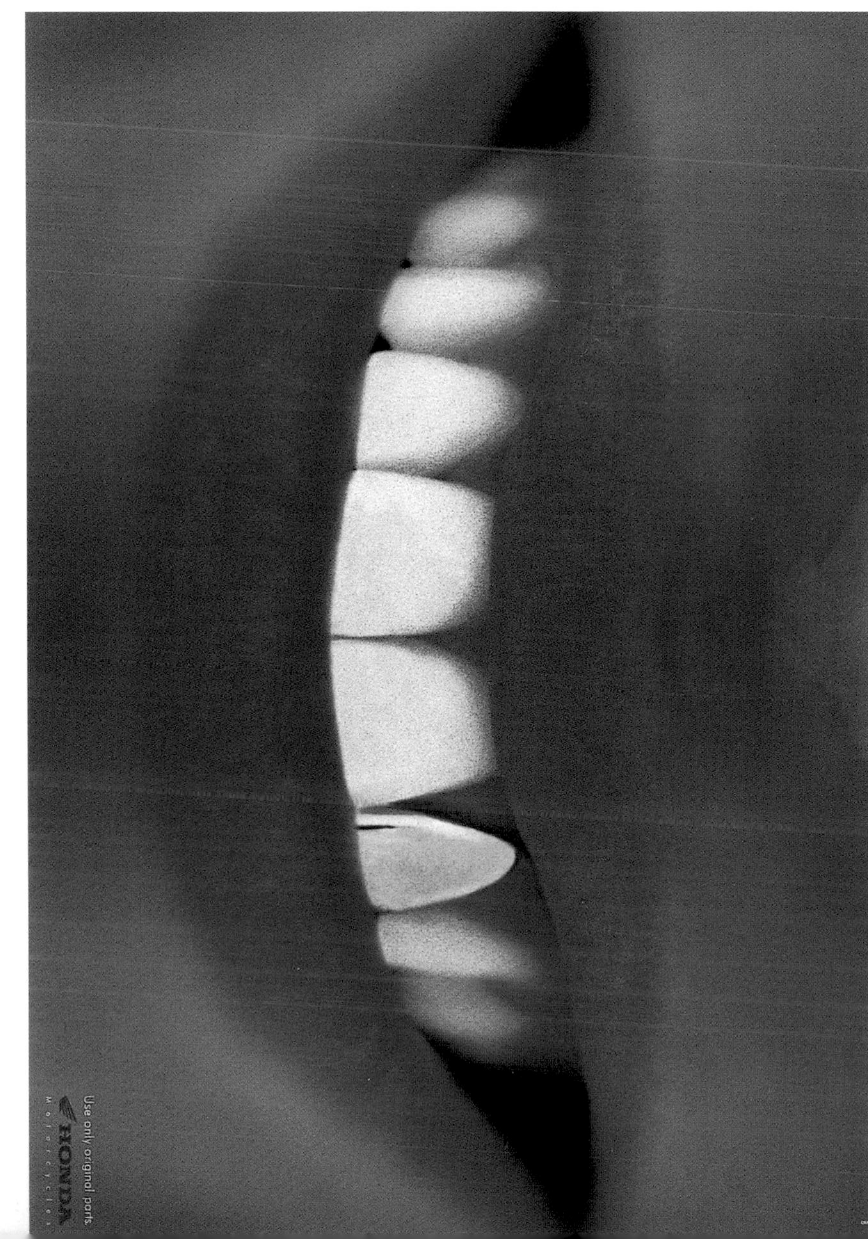
Use only original parts.
HONDA
Motorcycles

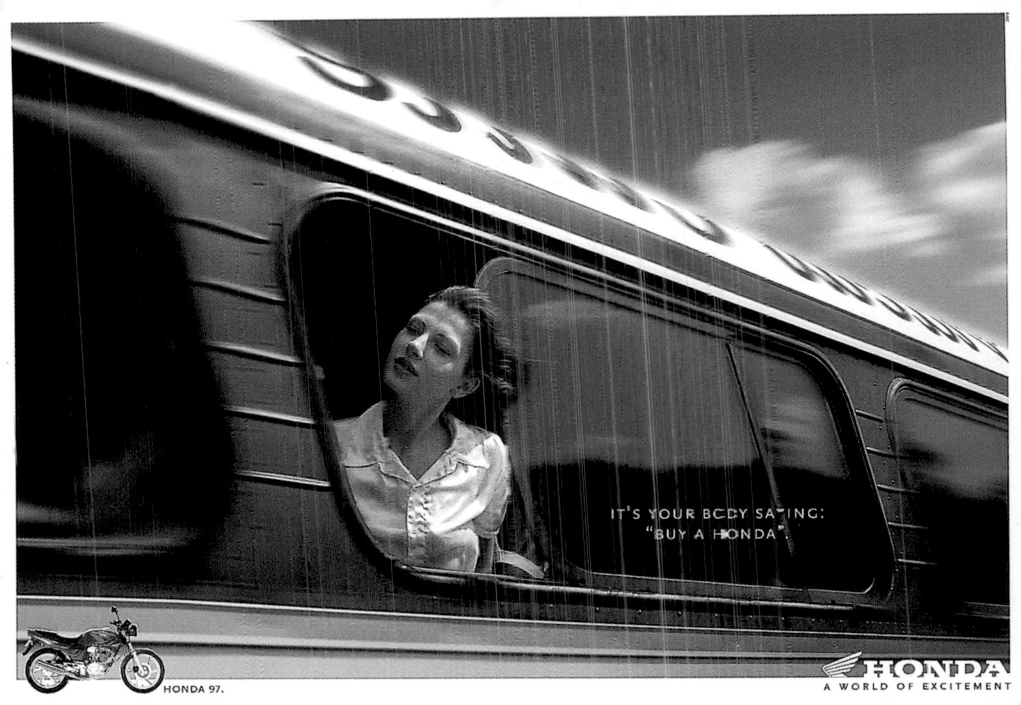
IT'S YOUR BODY SAYING:
"BUY A HONDA".
HONDA 97.
HONDA
A WORLD OF EXCITEMENT

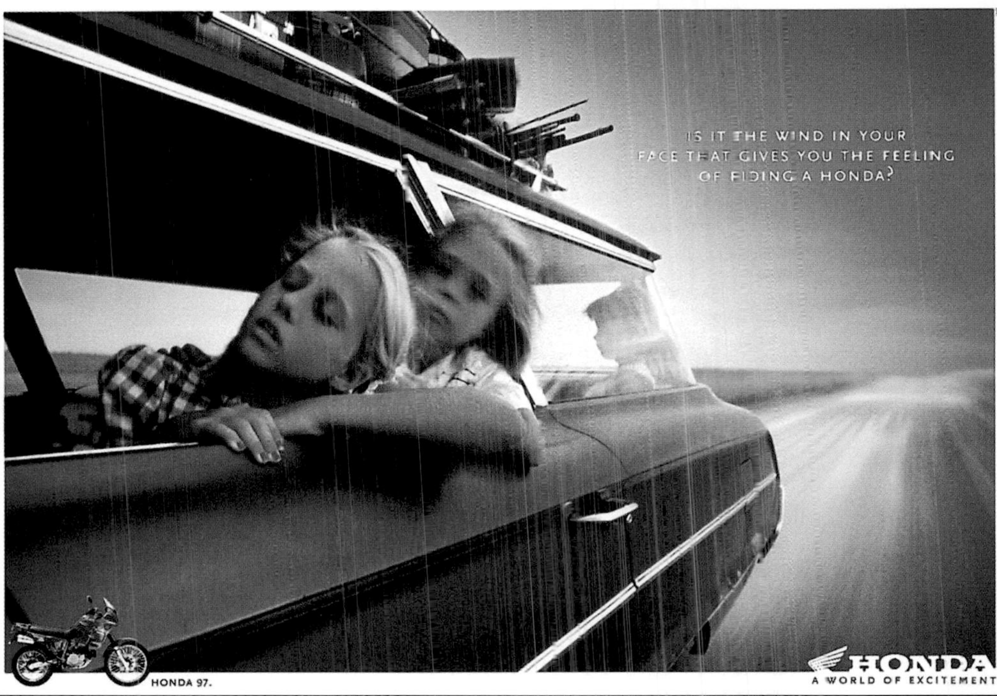
IS IT THE WIND IN YOUR
FACE THAT GIVES YOU THE FEELING
OF RIDING A HONDA?
HONDA 97.
HONDA
A WORLD OF EXCITEMENT

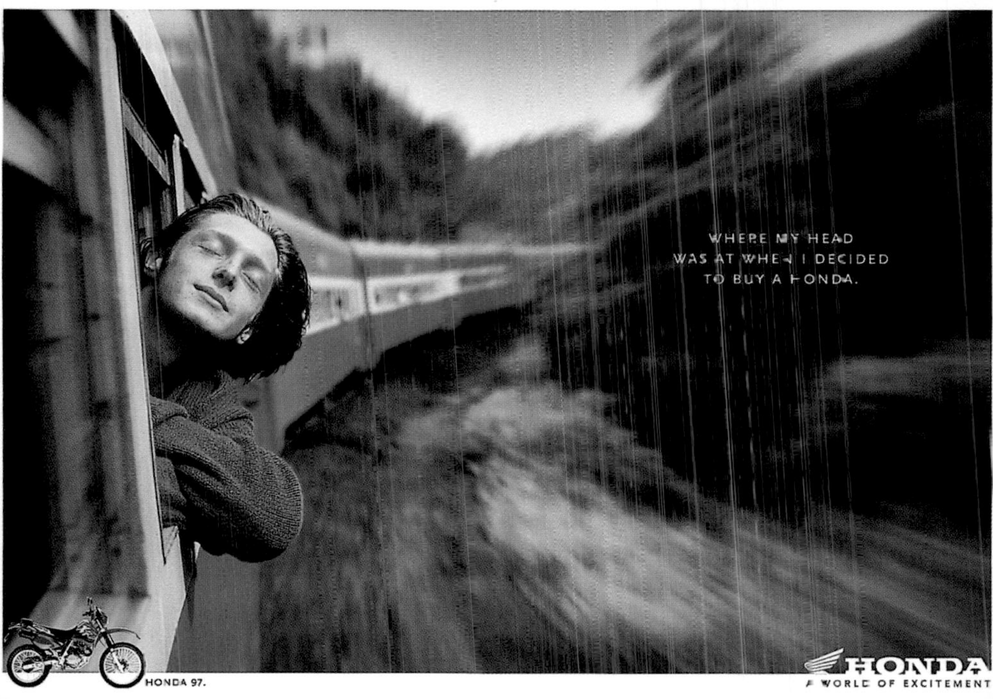
WHERE MY HEAD
WAS AT WHEN I DECIDED
TO BUY A HONDA.
HONDA 97.
HONDA
A WORLD OF EXCITEMENT

Client: Honda **Creative Directors:** Nizan Guanaes, Erh Ray, Camila Franco, Sergio Valente **Art Director:** Pedro Cappeletti **Copywriter:** Jader Rossetto **Account Executive:** Marcio Santoro **Photographer:** Arnaldo Pappalardo **Production:** Stacy Richards

His hair shows
that he's been dreaming
of the NX4 Falcon.

Introducing the NX4 Falcon.
The 400cc of your dreams.

They are dreaming of
the new NX4 Falcon.

Introducing the NX4 Falcon.
The 400cc of your dreams.

Another biker who
dreamed of the NX4 Falcon
all night long.

Introducing the NX4 Falcon.
The 400cc of your dreams.

Before
After
How to solve your big nose problem.
A ways wear a he met.
HONDA

Before
After
How to solve your hair loss problem.
Always wear a helmet.
HONDA

Client: Honda **Creative Director:** Tomás Lorente, Carlos Domingos **Art Director:** Pedro Cappeletti **Copywriter:** Jáder Rossetto **Account Executive:** Marcio Santoro **Photographer:** Fabio Bataglia

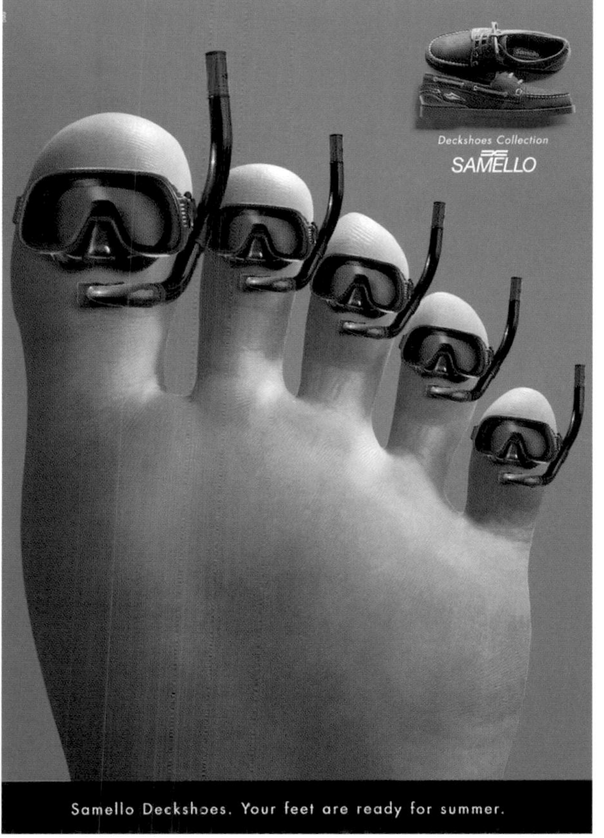

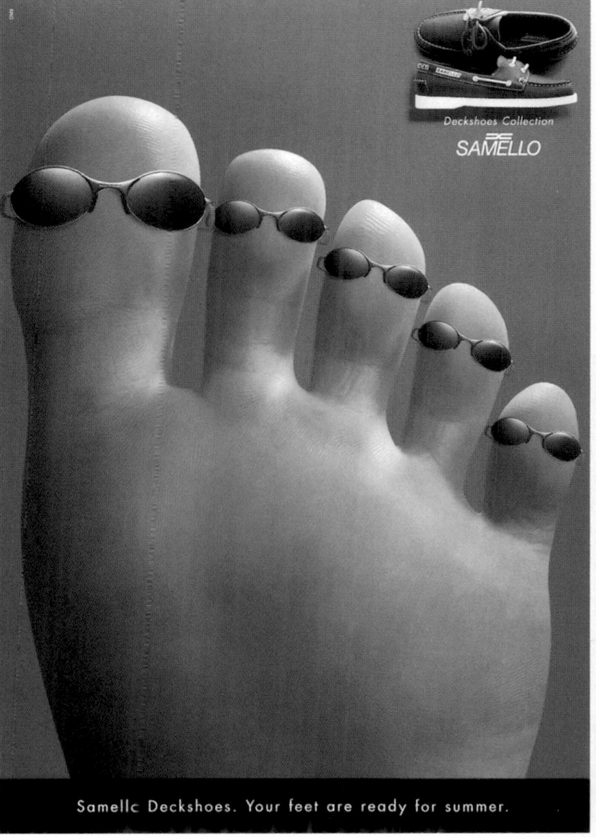

Client: (top) Esplanada Grill (bottom) Samello **Creative Directors:** Nizan Guanaes, Tomás Lorente **Art Director:** Pedro Cappeletti **Copywriter:** Jáder Rossetto **Account Executive:** Suely Ino **Photographer:** Paulo Vainer

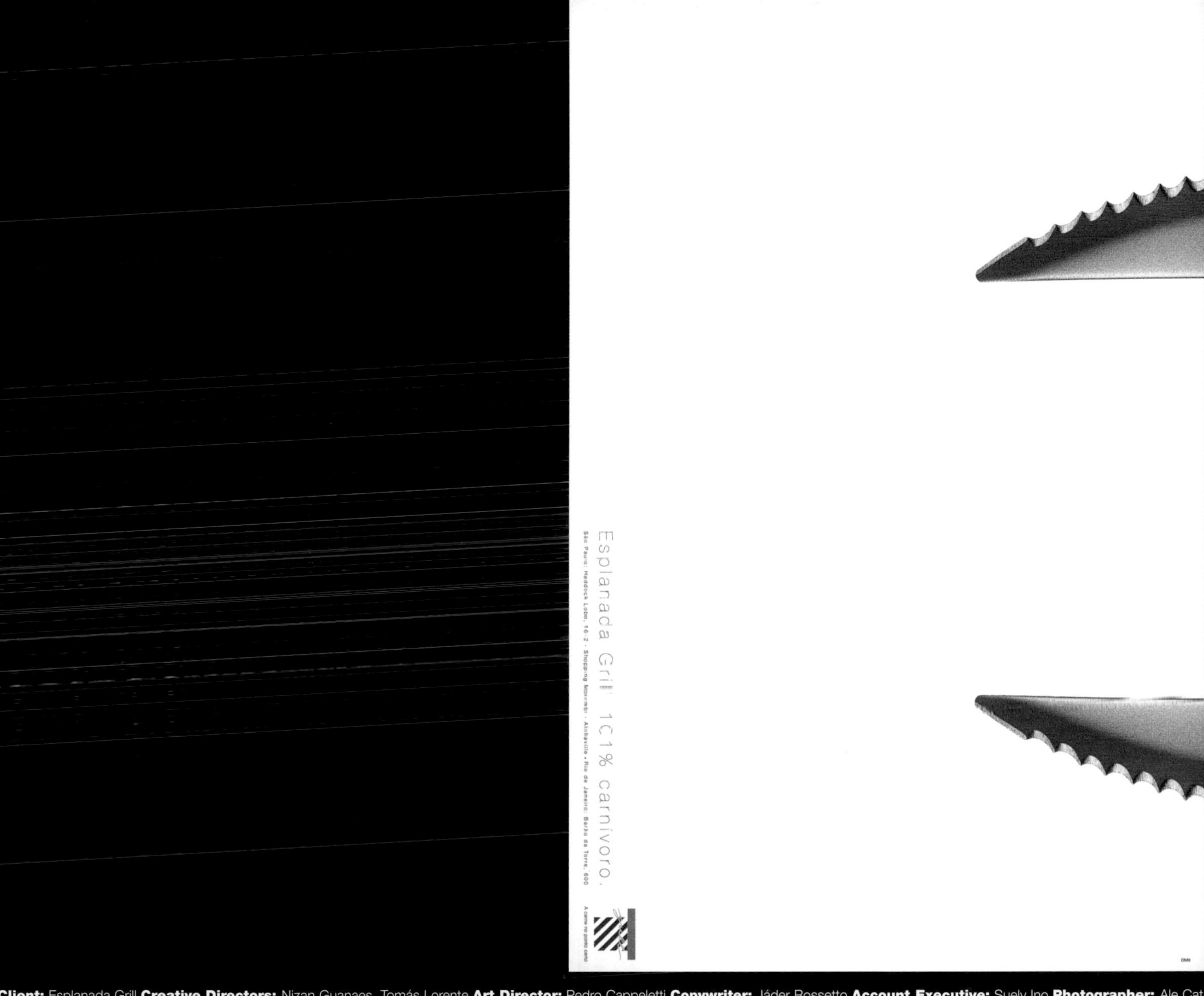

Client: Esplanada Grill **Creative Directors:** Nizan Guanaes, Tomás Lorente **Art Director:** Pedro Cappeletti **Copywriter:** Jáder Rossetto **Account Executive:** Suely Ino **Photographer:** Ale Cat

Botero
at the São Paulo
Museum of Art.
From March 17 to May 17

Client: São Paulo Museum of Art **Creative Directors:** Nizan Guanaes, Tomás Lorente **Art Director:** Pedro Cappeletti **Copywriter:** Jader Rossetto **Account Executive:** Graziela Araujo Opposite (top) **Client:** American Airlines **Creative Directors:** Carlos Domingos, Tomás Lorente **Art Director:** Mariana Sá **Copywriter:** Andrea Siqueira **Photographer:** Rafeal Costa

THE BEST OF HOLLYWOOD ON ALL AMERICAN AIRLINES FLIGHTS.
AmericanAirlines

Ops, I think I left the air-conditioner on.
Electrolux
The world leader in home appliances.
The coldest air-conditioner in the country.

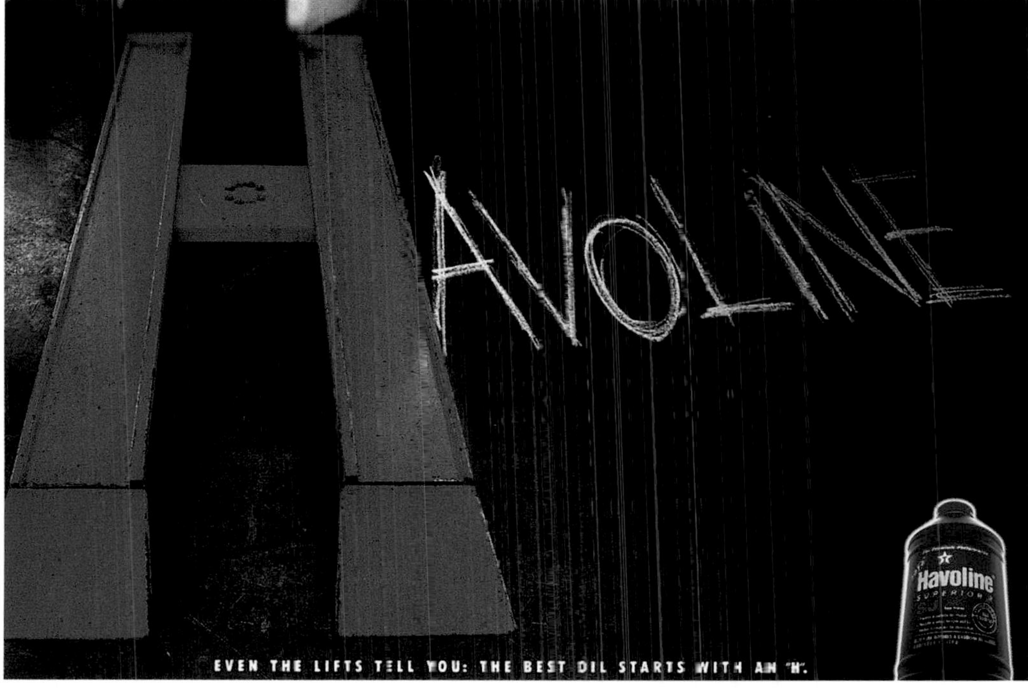
AVOLINE
EVEN THE LIFTS TELL YOU: THE BEST OIL STARTS WITH AN "H".
Havoline

(middle) **Client:** Electrolux **Creative Director:** Nizan Guanaes **Art Director:** Erh Ray **Copywriter:** José Enrique Borghi **Photographer:** Hakau Ludwigson (bottom) **Client:** Havoline **Creative Directors:** Nizan Guanaes, Tomás Lorente **Art Director:** Pedro Cappeletti **Copywriter:** Jáder Rossetto **Account Executive:** Segio Girard **Photographer:** Rodrigo Ribeiro

Page 30 *Diet Guarana Antarctica* In 1993, Brazil was honored, thanks to this ad, with its first Grand Prix at the Cannes Festival. This historic watershed brought Brazilian advertising worldwide recognition. And this ad, which had tremendous resonance, became a symbol of simplicity and the use of representative imagery for the ad industry. It also brought recognition for the work and dedication of DM9's creative team.

Page 31 *Itau Insurance* A good idea is one that translates the briefing in a creative way. In this campaign, we needed to say that now your car, your home and all your other possessions can be insured by phone. So simple that any more explaining would spoil it.

Page 32 *Parmalat* An image that makes consumers want to try the new Parmalat dessert. It could be a delicious photo of the dessert, it could be a child tasting the dessert, it could be a child eating the dessert and licking her lips. But then it wouldn't be here.

Page 33 *Parmalat* 4:00 pm—"How about food on fire? "6:00 pm—"How about a burnt toothbrush?" 6:01 pm—"I think I saw that one in some annual." 8:00pm—"How about a great big tongue?" 9:00 pm—"How about making the label a tongue?" 10:00 pm—"How about getting a pizza?" 11:00 pm—"How about getting some more time for this ad?" 12:00 am—"How about showing ketchup dripping down some kind of tongue?" 12:01 am—"Could be... write that down and we'll think some more."

Page 34 *Honda* A simple and efficient way to show how important it is to use original parts.

Page 35 *Honda* Freedom is a feeling that is difficult to describe. In this ad, our creatives found a simple way to translate the feeling: the wind blowing in your face. An emotional argument. The targets? Those who always wanted to have a motorcycle but their mothers wouldn't let them.

Page 36 *Honda* Could there be a more delightful way to show how nice it is to ride a motorcycle?

Page 37 *Honda* Sometimes rational safety arguments don't work. That's why we appealed to bikers' vanity.

Page 38 (top) *Espladada Grill* This ad plays with the idea that once you get in to Esplanada Grill restaurant , you'll never want to leave.
(bottom) *Samello* E o que os seus pés vão sentir quando não estão praticando mergulho? And what will your feet feel when they're not scuba diving?

Page 39 *Esplanada Grill* Thanks to the excellence of their product and to our previous campaigns, the Esplanada Grill had already consolidated its leadership in the steak house segment. This ad is just a little reminder of where to go when you feel like eating some meat.

Page 40 *São Paulo Museum of Art* This ad was such a hit around the world that we could claim only the nails that held Jesus to the cross are more famous than this one.

Page 41 *Havoline* This time, the client didn't even have to ask for their logo to be bigger. I don't know what the ramps for oil changes are like in your country, but in ours they're like an "H". That made it easy.

Av. Nações Unidas, 12901-36th Fl. Torre Norte, Centro Empresarial São Paulo, Brazil 04578-000 tel 5511-5501-9999 fax 5511-5103-0931

Fallon

To understand Fallon, you must first understand where it was born: In a city in the middle of the American Upper Midwestern prairie, where the summers are short, the winters are brutal and the work ethic comes straight off the farm—get up early, respect the people around you, stay humble, know you can always do better and never let your family down. Out of this came the remarkable vision to create the world's best advertising agency—an agency built not on the typical foundation of politics, competing agendas, inflated titles and expansive offices, but on a new model. ■ This model says that a great agency can outsmart the competition without outspending them. That brilliant creativity is an unfair advantage in the marketplace. That a creatively driven agency could have a strong business orientation and add economic value to big ideas. That a client list should be handpicked and small, so agency principals could stay neck-deep in client business. That an agency built around the work, and nothing but the work, could prosper. ■ It was founded in 1981 in Minneapolis as Fallon McElligott, by five people with more hopes than money, and an immediate goal of becoming a "national" agency. Fallon now bills almost $1 billion in Minneapolis, New York and London combined, and counts among its blue-chip client list some of the most impressive brands on the planet—brands that are no strangers to traditional marketing over promise, but have found in Fallon a relentless, kindred spirit where what matters is strategic and creative brilliance leading to marketplace results. ■ These brands include BMW, United Airlines, *TIME Magazine*, Nordstrom, Lee Jeans, Timex, Holiday Inn, Ralston Purina, Nikon, Starbucks, MTV, ABC Sports, Conseco, FAO Schwarz, BBC Radio, Budweiser and Skoda UK. They include famous campaigns, both old and new, such as the *Rolling Stone* "Perception/Reality," Prudential's "Be Your Own Rock," the Nuveen Investment's Christopher Reeve spot and Holiday Inn's "Mark" campaign. ■ Along the way, as Fallon won more creative awards in its short life than any other agency in the world, the focus of the company evolved from advertising to branding. Fallon's integrated approach to brand building is not only taught at many American universities, but also has helped attract new clients at the rate of 35% compound growth every year for the last five years. Fallon's creative excellence in design and new media has further solidified their ability to create integrated programs. ■ In February 2000, Fallon's reach grew exponentially as it became the second global network for the Publicis Groupe in France. Yet despite the growth, and despite the nascent internationalization of Fallon, the core values remain the same. It's still about the work, and nothing but the work. And the winters are still brutal.

pictured from left to right: Jamie Barrett, Executive Creative Director, Fallon New York; Fred Senn, Partner, Fallon Worldwide; Joe Duffy, Chairman, Duffy Worldwide; Alison Burns, President, Fallon New York; Pat Fallon, Chairman, Fallon Worldwide; Irv Fish, Chief Operating Officer, Fallon Worldwide; Rob White, President, Fallon Minneapolis; David Lubars, President/Executive Creative Director, Fallon Minneapolis; Michael Wall, Managing Partner, Fallon London.

Client: Nordstromshoes.com **Creative Director:** Peter McHugh **Art Director:** Scott O'Leary **Copywriter:** Michael Burdick **Account Executive:** Beth Perro Jarvis **Photographer:** John Clang

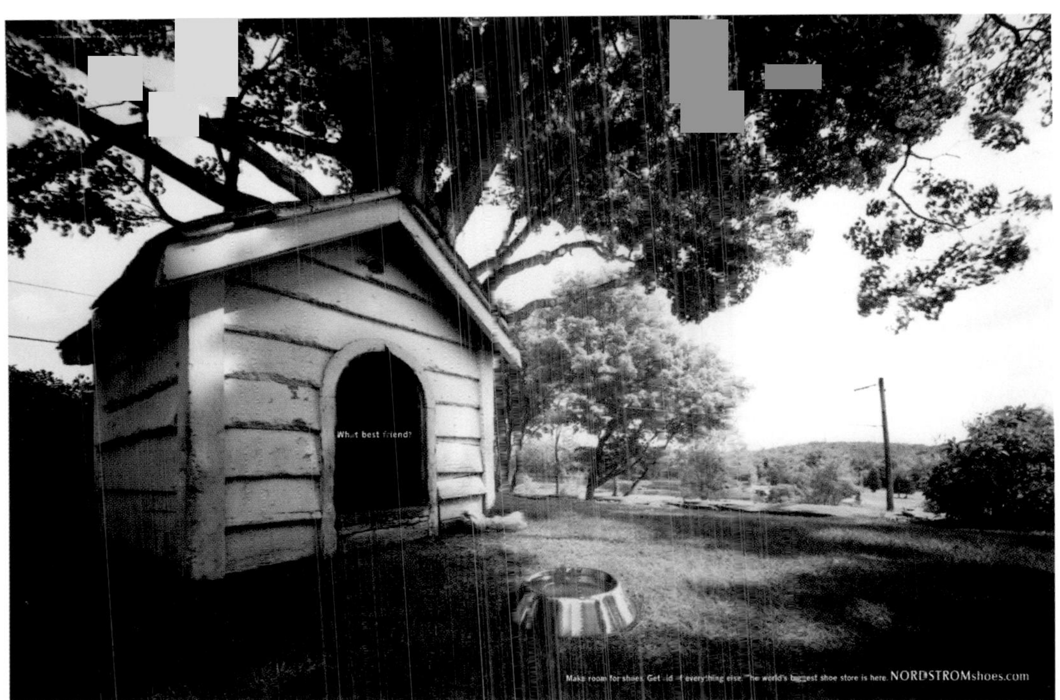
What best friend?
Make room for shoes. Get rid of everything else. The world's biggest shoe store is here. NORDSTROMshoes.com

How happily married are you?
Make room for shoes. Get rid of everything else. The world's biggest shoe store is here. NORDSTROMshoes.com

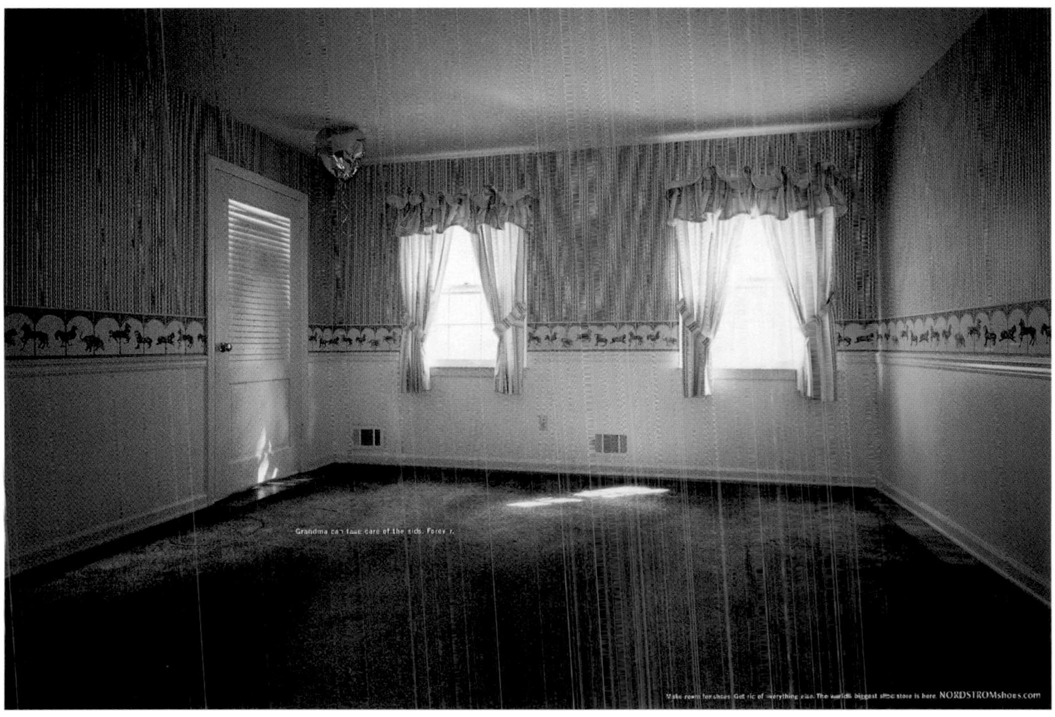
Grandma can take care of the kids. Forever.
Make room for shoes. Get rid of everything else. The world's biggest shoe store is here. NORDSTROMshoes.com

REinventTHE GIRL NEXT DOOR.
NORDSTROM
reinvent yourself

REinventSOCCER MOM.
NORDSTROM
reinvent yourself

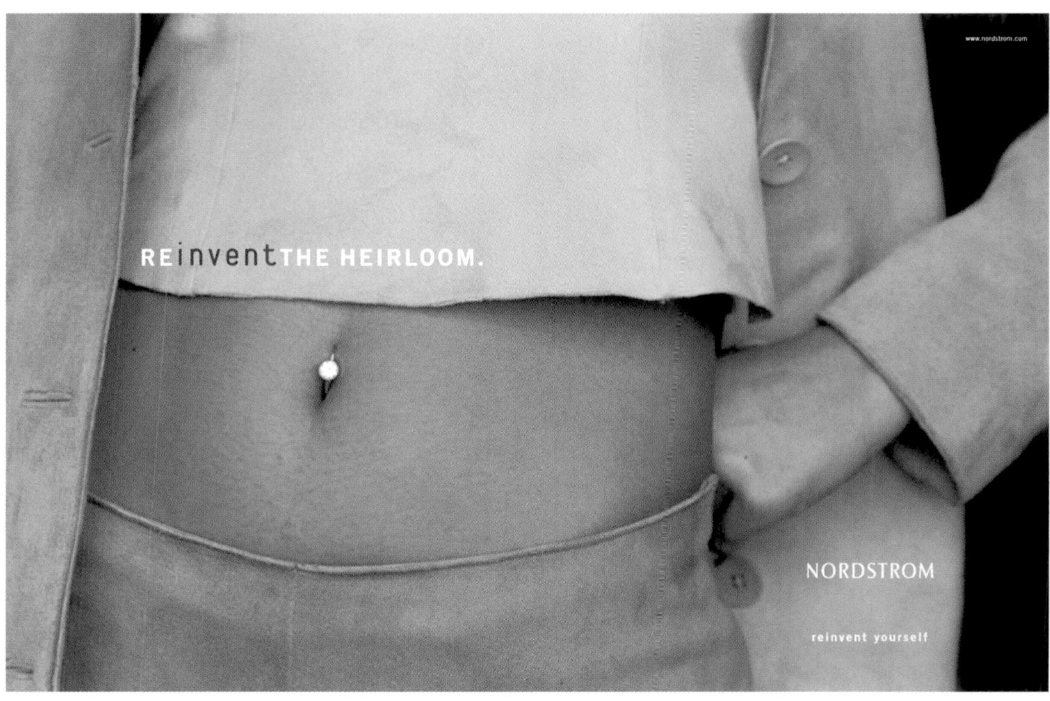
REinventTHE HEIRLOOM.
NORDSTROM
reinvent yourself

Client: Nordstrom **Creative Director:** Peter McHugh **Art Director:** Steve Driggs **Copywriter:** Nizan Guanaes **Account Executive:** Beth Perro Jarvis **Photographer:** William Abranowicz

Some photos have their own special beauty.

Here, the first transplanted hand.

The world's most interesting magazine.

Financial news, from the

budget deficit all the way up

to the Jagger settlement.

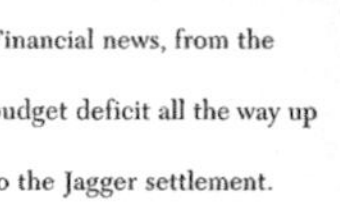

The world's most interesting magazine.

Insightful war correspondents.

Regrettably, still reporting.

The world's most interesting magazine.

A good story can make you

feel like you're there.

Or thank God that you're not.

The world's most interesting magazine.

Client: TIME Magazine **Creative Directors:** David Lubars, Jamie Barrett **Art Director:** Bob Barrie **Copywriter:** Dean Hanson **Account Executive:** Amy Frisch **Photographers:** Alexander Nemenov, Patrick Pfister, Stephanie Cardinale

Client: United Airlines **Creative Director:** Tom Lichtenheld **Art Director:** Dan Bryant **Copywriter:** Scott Cooney **Account Executive:** Tricia Davidson **Photographers:** Richard Hamilton Smith, David Harwood, Douglas Peebles

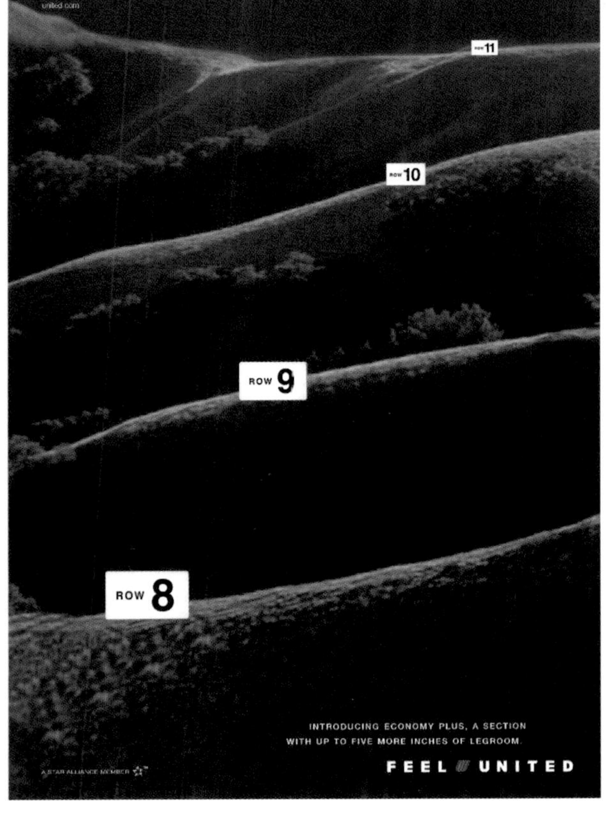

ROW 10
ROW 11
12
It's amazing what a few extra inches of space can feel like on an airplane.
Introducing Economy Plus, a new concept in seating from United. By removing a row of seats from our planes, we're creating
sections with three to five more inches of legroom per seat. The program has already started, and will be in place in the
majority of our U.S. fleet by April of 2000. Soon, you'll be experiencing wide-open spaces before you even leave the ground.
UNITED

Client: Sports Illustrated **Creative Director:** David Lubars **Art Director:** Steve Driggs **Designer:** Jason Strong **Copywriter:** Greg Hahn **Account Executive:** Kevin Berigan **Photographers:** Carl Skalak, Aubrey Washington, David E. Klutho, John W. McDonough

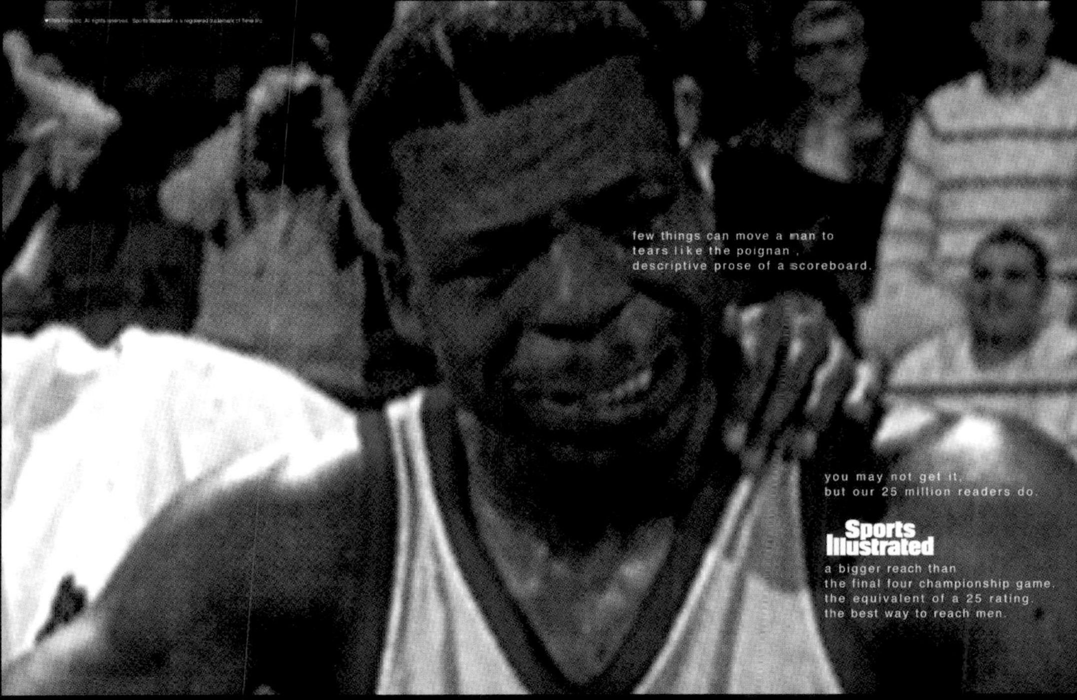

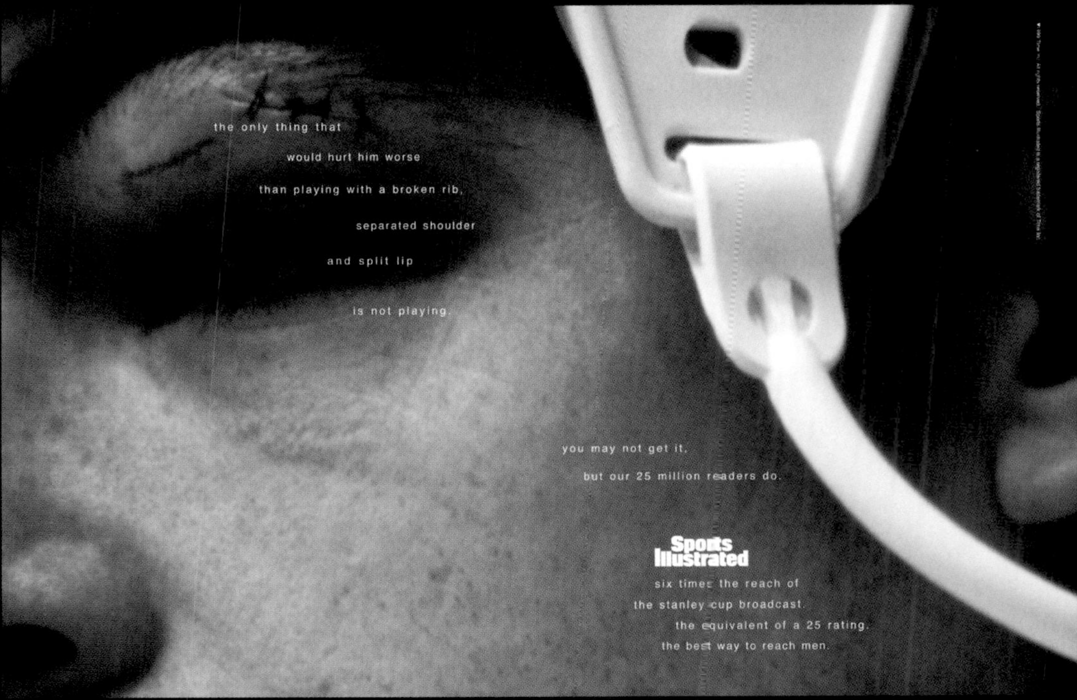

few things can move a man to
tears like the poignan ,
descriptive prose of a scoreboard.

you may not get it,
but our 25 million readers do.

Sports Illustrated

a bigger reach than
the final four championship game.
the equivalent of a 25 rating.
the best way to reach men.

the only thing that
would hurt him worse
than playing with a broken rib,
separated shoulder
and split lip
is not playing.

you may not get it,
but our 25 million readers do.

Sports Illustrated

six times the reach of
the stanley cup broadcast.
the equivalent of a 25 rating.
the best way to reach men.

THERE'S A 95 MPH PROJECTILE
SCREAMING TOWARD HIS FACE.
AND THE ONLY THING HE'S AFRAID OF
IS THAT IT MIGHT NOT HIT HIM.
YOU MAY NOT GET IT,
BUT OUR 25 MILLION READERS DO.
Sports Illustrated
ROY
33

LEFT
OR RIGHT?
THIS IS
WHAT WILL
DETERMINE
THE HAPPINESS
OF THOUSANDS
OF OTHERWISE
WELL-ADJUSTED
PEOPLE.
YOU MAY NOT GET IT.
BUT OUR 25 MILLION
READERS DO.
Sports Illustrated

lucky sock.
bought jan. 16.
worn jan. 17.
worn jan. 19.
worn jan. 27.
worn jan. 28.
worn feb. 1.
worn feb. 3.
worn feb. 4.
worn feb. 10
worn feb. 12
worn feb. 14.
worn feb. 16.
worn feb. 18.
worn mar. 1.
worn mar. 3.
worn mar. 4.
worn mar. 6.
worn mar. 7.
worn mar. 9.
worn mar. 11.
worn mar. 13.
worn mar. 15.
worn mar. 16.
worn mar. 18.
worn apr. 3.
worn apr. 5.
worn apr. 7.
worn apr. 8.
washed apr. 9.
you may not get it.
but our 25 million readers do.
Sports Illustrated
a bigger reach than
game 6 of the nba finals.
the equivalent of a 25 rating.
the best way to reach men.

Dynamic Stability Control
Dynamic Brake Control
All Season Traction
Variable Valve Timing
4-Wheel Antilock Brakes
Impact Sensor
Head Protection System
GPS Navigation System
Safety Belt Pretensioners
Side-impact Airbags
Side Door Anchoring
Park Distance Control
Better visibility
Xenon Headlights
Dual Threshold Airbags
Xenon headlights, introduced by BMW in 1993, operate on the same principle as high-powered stadium lights to provide exceptional night vision. Visit www.bmwusa.com or call 1-800-334-4BMW.

The Ultimate Driving Machine®

Dynamic Brake Control
All Season Traction
Variable Valve Timing
4-Wheel Antilock Brakes
Impact Sensor
Head Protection System
GPS Navigation System
Safety Belt Pretensioners
Side-impact Airbags
Side Door Anchoring
Park Distance Control
Xenon Headlights
Better cornering
Dynamic Stability Control
Dual Threshold Airbags
BMW's ingenious Dynamic Stability Control gives you remarkable control while cornering or for quick maneuvers in an emergency. Visit www.bmwusa.com or call 1-800-334-4BMW.
The Ultimate Driving Machine®

Dynamic Stability Control
Dynamic Brake Control
Variable Valve Timing
4-Wheel Antilock Brakes
Impact Sensor
Head Protection System
GPS Navigation System
Safety Belt Pretensioners
Side-impact Airbags
Side Door Anchoring
Park Distance Control
Xenon Headlights
Better grip
All Season Traction
Dual Threshold Airbags
BMW's All Season Traction controls engine torque and rear brakes to virtually eliminate wheelspin for exceptional confidence on rainy or snowy surfaces. Visit www.bmwusa.com or call 1-800-334-4BMW.
The Ultimate Driving Machine®

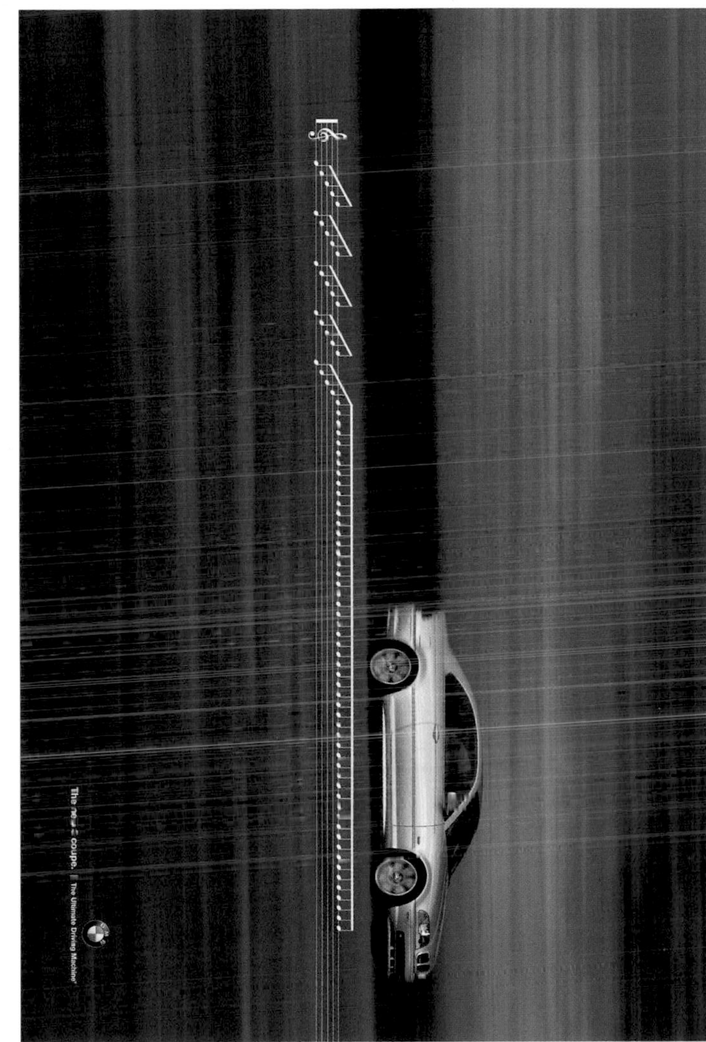

Client: BMW of North America **Creative Directors:** Bruce Bildsten, Tom Lichtenheld **Art Director:** David Carter **Copywriter:** Joe Sweet **Account Executive:** Ginny Grossman **Photographer:** Clint Clemens

I LOVE YOU, TOO.

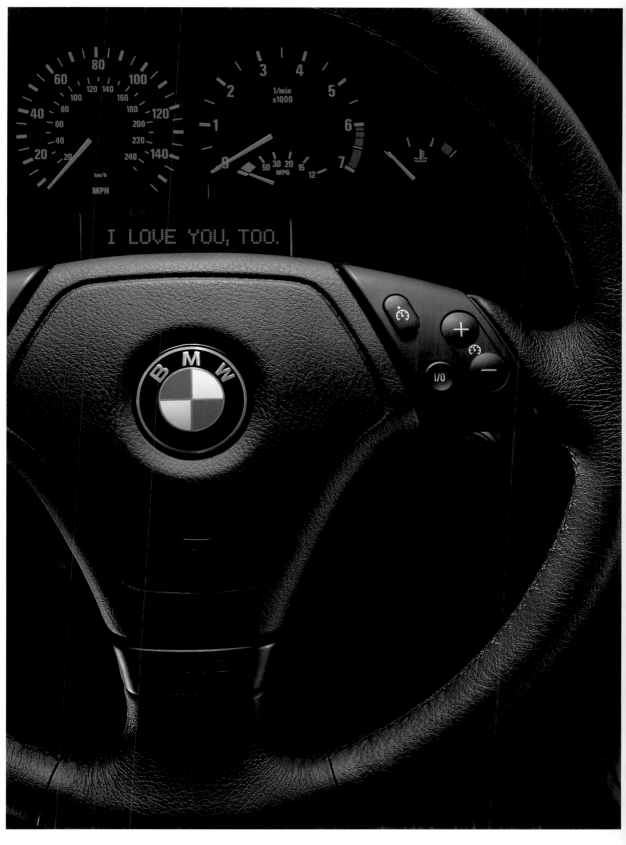

Client: BMW of North America **Creative Directors:** Bruce Bildsten, Tom Lichtenheld **Art Director:** Steve Sage **Copywriter:** Joe Sweet **Account Executive:** Ginny Grossman **Photographer:** Mark LaFavor

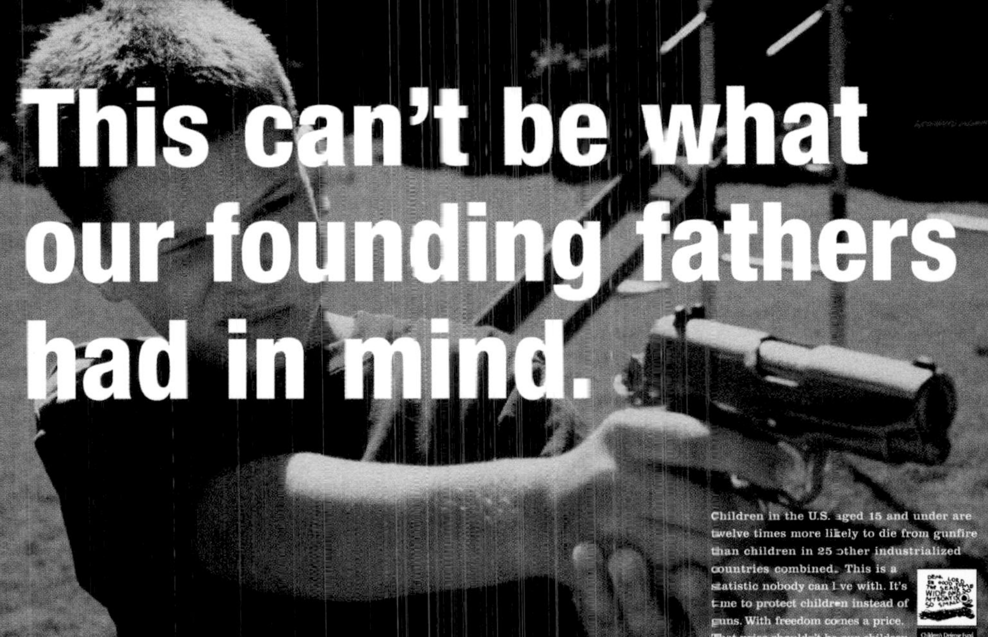

This can't be what our founding fathers had in mind.
Children in the U.S. aged 15 and under are twelve times more likely to die from gunfire than children in 25 other industrialized countries combined. This is a statistic nobody can live with. It's time to protect children instead of guns. With freedom comes a price. That price shouldn't be our children.
Children's Defense Fund
1-800-CDF-1200 or www.childrensdefense.org

Kids in trench coats shoot up school. The response? Ban trench coats.

It's time to stop the posturing, the politicking, the endless debating. Nearly 13 children die from gunfire each day in America. Until we get guns out of the hands of children, children will die at the hands of guns. Let's deal with the real issues. It's time we protect children instead of guns.

Children's Defense Fund®

1-800-CDF-1200 or www.childrensdefense.org

Remember when the only thing kids were afraid of at school was a pop quiz?

We live in a time when children have to pass through metal detectors before they go to math class. 33% of children polled believe an incident similar to the one in Littleton would occur in their school. Peace of mind is a cruel victim of random violence. And one we can't afford to lose. Support stricter gun legislation. It's time we protect children instead of guns.

Children's Defense Fund®

1-800-CDF-1200 or www.childrensdefense.org

POLICE

Page 46-47 *Nordstromshoes.com* Nordstrom has set the benchmark for service over the years, a brand highly admired by customers, vendors, and dedicated employees. Becoming the biggest shoe store online would require refocusing their existing e-commerce strategy to drive sales. Their site was launched in 1998 with little consumer marketing support. In spring of 1999, there was a strong desire to get communications out into the marketplace as soon as possible, and to support seasonal retail pushes. This approach supported tactical opportunities as opposed to a core strategic focus. And funds were limited. It was a natural to make this bold move in a new forum—online. We created a strategic platform that maximized impact and drove traffic and sales. On November 1, 1999, NordstromShoes.com—the world's biggest online shoe store—was launched with TV, print, OOH and PR. Results were immediate and impressive. Shoe sales increased 33% in the first month. Shoes account for 40% of all Nordstrom online sales. Media coverage of the work and the site strategy in business and consumer print has been outstanding. Driven by the campaign and news coverage, NordstromShoes.com is also experiencing record per day online sales of items other than shoes.

Page 48 *Nordstrom* As Nordstrom looked to its future, there was no way this great brand would risk becoming "just another department store." The turn of a new millennium was the time to rededicate themselves to reenergizing the brand, to make a great brand even greater. An 18 month strategic process laid the groundwork for an all-inclusive brand strategy and repositioning effort. No stone was left unturned—from the dot.com side to full-line store strategies. From the store experience and navigation to the communications plan. The result is an evolved specialty apparel retail brand that really delivers on the notion of a "reinvented" shopping experience, for shoppers who are looking to reinvent themselves a bit, too.

Page 49 *TIME Magazine* TIME Magazine was a mature brand in a category whose very existence was being threatened by an influx of new media news sources. In fact, the three leaders of the category had been referred to as dinosaurs of a dying industry. We needed to reinforce and reinvigorate the brand's essence of insight, analysis, and perspective, and maximize profitability through increased subscriber retention among TIME's most important customers. We launched a brand campaign for TIME that highlighted its unique ability to bring analysis and perspective to the events that shape the world. The campaign's successes have not been limited to creative accolades (although it has, among other awards, been named "Best Print Campaign of the Decade" by the One Club). As a result, TIME has experienced the strongest renewal rates of any magazine in its category, made significant improvement in audience composition across its most profitable demos, and been named "Magazine of the Year" by Advertising Age for two of the past three years.

Page 50-51 *United Airlines* In 1978, airline deregulation led to declining revenues and cost cutting, which, in turn, led to decreased customer service. Consumers began to choose carriers based on schedule convenience, ticket prices, and perks rather than an emotional affinity toward any airline. United was no different, and their customers noticed. As such, their long-standing "Friendly Skies" campaign became inaccurate and irrelevant, particularly for frequent business travelers. In 1995, United shifted its focus from a transportation company to a service brand, aiming to develop a loyal, high-yield consumer base. In 1997, they came to Fallon. In order to succeed, United had to first find a relevant, differentiating message that increased consumer preference and reestablished its leadership position, and second, rally the 95,000 United employees to get behind the message and work to deliver on its promise. The initial approach, the "Rising" campaign, was successful in raising awareness and consumer preference (to number one overall), but the industry quickly followed United's lead in acknowledging the need for improvement. This latest challenge was to evolve the message once again. In addition to communicating the scope of service and products from United, we would also focus overtly on who United is—the strength of its culture—to help the consumer, and the employee, understand why they do what they do. This campaign added conviction to United's restored reputation, focusing on a very specific, tangible motivation—being United to create a better journey.

Page 52-53 Sports Illustrated: Sports Illustrated competes with every media vehicle that targets men—including big-budget ads for television. Our challenge was to convince advertisers that Sports Illustrated was a viable alternative to network and cable sports television. We uncovered two key insights that ultimately led to our creative strategy: 1) In an effort to reach a large quantity of men, advertisers and media planners often think of sports, and generally equate sports with television. 2) Advertisers and media planners were getting fed up with the networks over sports negotiations—the prices were going up and the rules were tightening while the ratings continued to fall off. We created the "SI Option"—to convince our target that Sports Illustrated was a legitimate alternative to sports television. We didn't do it with spreadsheets and numbers; a rational argument alone wasn't going to change a long-standing paradigm. We enabled media planners to see Sports Illustrated the way our readers see it. The fact is that Sports Illustrated has 25 million passionately involved readers who look to SI as the authority on sports. For these readers, Sports Illustrated picks up where TV leaves off, bringing them deeper inside the stories they've seen unfold. Our creative strategy was to communicate this powerful relationship. And the Advertisers responded. Wendy's restaurants was exclusively a broadcast advertiser prior to learning about the SI Option. Other major advertisers were soon to follow—K-Mart, Miller Lite, and Compaq, to name a few. Sports Illustrated is currently enjoying its sixth consecutive year of double-digit ad revenue growth.

Page 54 *BMW of North America* In 1997, BMW was in danger of losing its long-standing lead in the import luxury car segment, and furthermore, its brand position as a high-performance vehicle. Unlike Mercedes, Lexus and Audi, which were all coming on strong with great new products and new marketing campaigns designed to dethrone BMW, the brand was not about luxury—it was about being fun to drive. As consumer rankings for attributes like "fun to drive" and "responsive handling." fell to virtually the same level as Mercedes or Lexus, it was clear to BMW drivers and retailers that BMW drivers had very different ways than competitive drivers of describing what "fun to drive" meant. Competitive drivers used very simplistic terms, like "drive really fast" or "stop on a dime." BMW drivers used a much richer vocabulary, talking about "feeling at one with the car," "hugging the corner," and "the feeling of exhilaration when you step on the gas." They spoke of maneuvering, handling, braking, and passing, as well as accelerating. In the BMW driver's mind, their cars didn't just drive faster than the competition, they were more responsive. It occurred to us that competitive drivers had no idea what they were missing. The creative challenge was to show consumers that what their car does well a BMW does brilliantly. To achieve this objective we created a brand campaign in the point-of-view style, to give a sense of what it's like behind the wheel of a BMW. We also touted specific new models such as the 3 Series sedans, coupes, sport wagon, and convertible, and the X5 Sports Activity Vehicle. BMW's association with James Bond in the movies "Tomorrow Never Dies" and "The World Is Not Enough" further reinforced the performance message. Finally, we leveraged BMW's participation in motorsports as additional proof of the brand's performance authenticity.

Page 55 *BMW of North America* The launch of the BMW 3 Series coupe was important in introducing a redesigned version of one of the most popular BMWs on the road. Its refined, expressive aesthetics and equally refined yet potent performance needed to draw to a wide range of enthusiasts. The communications needed to reflect the youthful, independent statement that is, in essence, the new 3 Series coupe. Importantly, the creative needed to be dynamic, fresh and exhilarating.

Page 56 *BMW of North America* BMW designs its automobiles with focus on performance and driving passion. In 1998, the BMW family grabbed the attention of critics and received several awards including Car and Driver's "10 Best Cars" for the M coupe, M3 and 5 Series cars. Eight models throughout the BMW family received high praise creating an impressive message worth sharing. The challenge was to create an accolade ad that felt like an extension of the brand campaign and wasn't overtly boastful. The photography is a beautiful family portrait showcasing the award-winning models and their accolades. "I Love You Too" is a message of thanks to loyal owners affirming that the car loves the driver as much as the driver loves the car; a direct tie-in to the overall brand statement.

Page 57 *Children's Defense Fund* On the heels of the devastating shootings in Columbine, the Children's Defense Fund asked Fallon to assist in its efforts to limit children's access to guns. The goal: to convince all parties concerned with the gun debate that limiting children's access to guns was undeniably necessary and indeed possible. We needed to shift the focus of the gun debate from its complicated web of politics and emotions to one overarching goal: the safety of our nation's children. The campaign resulting from this strategy employed CDF's trademark tone: direct and hard-hitting, designed to prompt immediate debate and action on this issue before the next senseless tragedy occurred. Such provocative statements and questions raised eyebrows. We got people thinking, and responding. And we placed the ultimate question in people's minds across the country: "How many more lives do we have to lose before we say enough is enough?"

Goodby, Silverstein & Partners

Goodby, Silverstein & Partners

For better or worse, the place is impossible to copy. Things happen here that don't happen at other advertising companies. ■ Today, Beau Bouverat is devising a camera that can be dropped from the top of a building, just to see what it feels like to jump off. Claude Shade is unhappy with some Photoshop degraded type, so he's finishing it with a wood-burner. Jessica Gath in our planning department has just opened a show of her paintings in our art gallery. Tom Miller is using a pocket fisherman to lower ten dollar bills onto the California Street sidewalk, where he moves them just as the tourists try to pick them up. Goodby is learning how to make mannequins look like they're drinking beer for an upcoming Budweiser shoot. And Silverstein is meticulously piecing together a face from ripped up magazine photos. ■ Such random experimentation and amusement has somehow resulted in what may be the most diversely successful advertising agency since the early days of Doyle Dane Bernbach. In less than two decades, Goodby, Silverstein & Partners has done more widely recognized work, for more different clients, than any other agency in the world. ■ In the New York One Club's retrospective show on the best advertising of the 1990s, we were by far the most represented company. We've been Agency of the Year in *Advertising Age* (twice) and *Adweek*, and also in *Shoot*, *Business 2.0* and *Modern Computing*. On *USA Today*'s top 10 list of the All-time most remembered campaigns, three were ours—more than any other agency. TV Guide picked our Bud lizards campaign as the best of the '90s. And we've won every major award in advertising (most of them several times over), including the Palm d'Or at Cannes and Agency of the Year at the Clio Awards. ■ Aside from winning notoriety for campaigns such as "got milk?," E*Trade, Budweiser, Nike, Polaroid, Norwegian Cruise Line, Porsche and Sega, GS&P has also devised some of the most innovative techniques and ideas of the past few decades. We were one of the first agencies (if not the first) to use 8mm film and degraded video tape extensively in our work. We used the first cameras hidden in people's clothing to get unvarnished consumer responses. We shot spots that threw real people and actors together with no scripts whatsoever. For Chevy's Mexican Restaurants, we shot commercials, ran them, and threw them away—all in the same day, the way the restaurant made its food. ■ As we head into the next decade of this stuff, it occurs to us that, just as we hoped, advertising will become more and more like performance art. No longer constricted to 30 seconds or a single page size, it will be liberated to do long form, expansive things unheard of today. It will sneak up on you, big-time. ■ We feel we will be well-prepared for this new world, because so much of what we've done is already predicated on such unexpectedness. We feel we have brought to our communications an unusual respect for the end user. And we have embraced advertising as art in service to business, as a creation that is impossible to avoid—like architecture or landscape design—one that necessitates an environmentally-conscious approach. Treat people at their best; assume they have a sense of humor; involve them at higher levels in what you have to say. The rest will take care of itself.

Portrait of Jeff Goodby (left) and Rich Silverstein (right) by Mel Lindstrom

Client: Sonicare **Creative Director:** Steve Simpson **Art Director:** Sean Farrell **Copywriter:** Chris Ford **Account Executive:** Erika Mielke **Photographers:** John Gipe, Mika Manninen

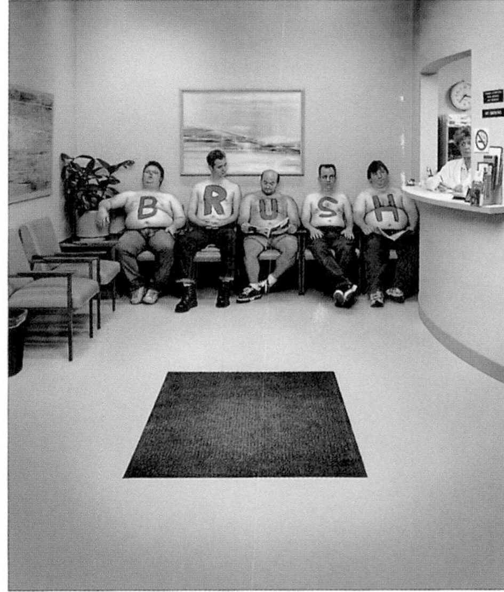

Note to dentists:
Be careful what you wish for.

The sonicare sonic toothbrush cleans with a combination of 31,000 brush strokes per minute and gentle sonic waves. sonicare also removes nearly twice as much plaque between teeth as a manual toothbrush. It's a one-two punch that gives your patients a clean feeling so unique, it'll turn just about anyone into a dental hygiene fanatic. In fact, we'll even guarantee your patients better checkups after just 90 days, or we'll give them their money back.

sonicare
It's not just a better toothbrush.
It's a better checkup.

Has a patient of yours ever
gotten this excited about dental hygiene?

The sonicare sonic toothbrush cleans with a combination of 31,000 brush strokes per minute and gentle sonic waves. sonicare also removes nearly twice as much plaque between teeth as a manual toothbrush. It's a one-two punch that gives your patients a clean feeling so unique, it'll turn just about anyone into a dental hygiene fanatic. In fact, we'll even guarantee your patients better checkups after just 90 days, or we'll give them their money back.

sonicare
It's not just a better toothbrush.
It's a better checkup.

CHAMOIS FLEECE ●●●●● BEARS HAVE FUR. WHALES HAVE BLUBBER. YOU HAVE THIS.

nike.com/fleece

DRI-FIT BASE LAYER ●●●●● WICKS AWAY SWEAT. ATTRACTS STARES.

nike.com/baselayer

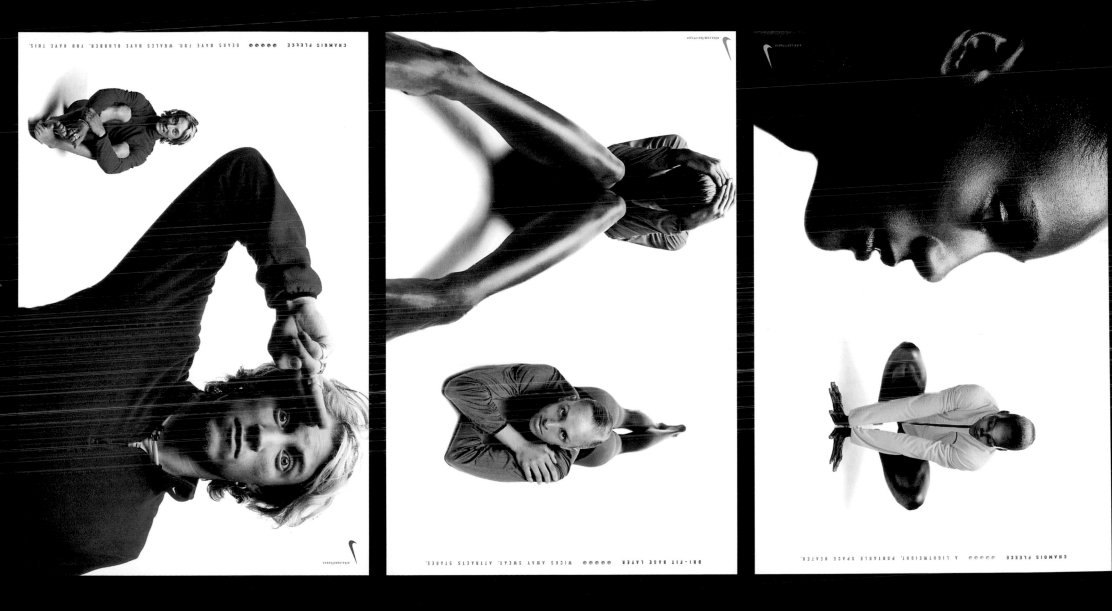

CHAMOIS FLEECE ●●●●● A LIGHTWEIGHT, PORTABLE SPACE HEATER.

nike.com/fleece

Client: Nike **Creative Directors:** Jeff Goodby, Rich Silverstein **Art Director:** Margaret Johnson **Copywriter:** Steve Payonzeck **Account Executive:** Darren Brady-Harris **Photographer:** Thierry LeGoues **Production Artist:** Mark Rurka

Client: Beaver Creek Resort **Creative Directors:** Rich Silverstein, Steve Simpson **Art Director:** Rich Silverstein **Copywriter:** Steve Simpson **Account Executive:** Lynn Woodward **Illustrator:** David McMacken **Production:** Stacy Richards, Max Fallo

NORTH AMERICA'S GRAND MOUNTAIN RESORT™
Beaver Creek VILLAGE
COLORADO
SKI-IN-LODGING·PERFORMING ARTS·BOUTIQUES·DINING

NORTH AMERICA'S GRAND MOUNTAIN RESORT™
ALT. 11,440 FT.
WORLD CHAMPIONSHIP BIRDS OF PREY DOWNHILL
BEAVER CREEK
COLORADO

NORTH AMERICA'S GRAND MOUNTAIN RESORT™
WORLD
FAMOUS
CHILDREN'S
SKI
SCHOOL
COLORADO
BEAVER CREEK
A GREAT FAMILY TRADITION

BEAVER CREEK COLORADO
GOLF · HIKING · MOUNTAIN BIKING
RAFTING · FLY FISHING · TENNIS
ALT. 11,440
NORTH AMERICA'S GRAND MOUNTAIN RESORT

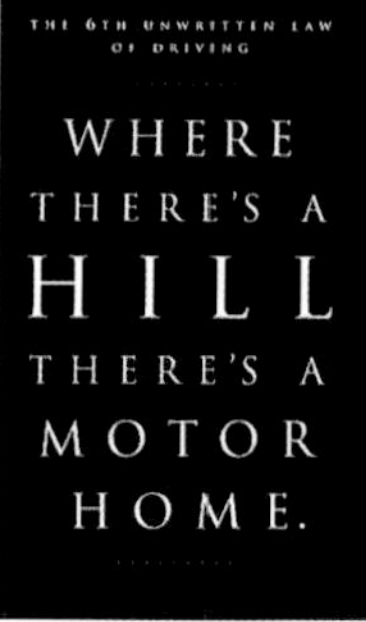

THE 6TH UNWRITTEN LAW OF DRIVING
WHERE THERE'S A HILL THERE'S A MOTOR HOME.

The new Isuzu Trooper has been thoughtfully redesigned to include a powerful 190 horse, dual overhead cam, 24-valve V6 engine,* which can eat up a stretch of highway pretty quick. Even that steep part. You know, the one that every slow moving vehicle in the world knows you're going to be on so they go there just to irritate you? Well, dust'em with that new Trooper of yours.

ISUZU
Practically/Amazing

THE 58TH UNWRITTEN LAW OF DRIVING

THE ROAD IS PAVED WITH IDIOTS.

UNLIKE MOST 4WD VEHICLES DUAL AIR BAGS COME STANDARD

HIGH GROUND CLEARANCE FOR A BETTER OVERALL VIEW

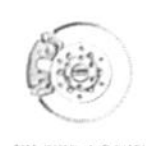
THE ONLY 4WD WITH STANDARD 4 WHEEL VENTILATED DISC ABS BRAKES

IMPACT ABSORBING STRUCTURE DESIGNED TO PROTECT THE CABIN

HEAD LAMP WIPERS CLEARLY A BENEFIT ESPECIALLY IN MUD

They're out there, those runners of stop signs, those no-signal lane changers. And while we can do little to stop them, we've gone to great lengths to make them less of a threat. Presenting the new Trooper Limited. For more information please call (800) 726-2700.

ISUZU
Practically/Amazing

THE 9TH UNWRITTEN LAW OF DRIVING

THE ATTRACTION OF SHOPPING CARTS TO AUTOMOBILES IS AMONG THE STRONGEST FORCES IN THE UNIVERSE.

This being the way of things, we give every new Trooper five coats of tough shopping cart-resistant, space-aged stuff. Then we paint the parts only the road sees four times. Nine coats in all. Then we bake it. Because even with a 190 horse dual overhead cam engine* and rear multi-link/coil suspension, a parked Trooper must be able to survive shopping carts, artistic birds and the car doors of those who long to be close to you.

ISUZU
Practically/Amazing

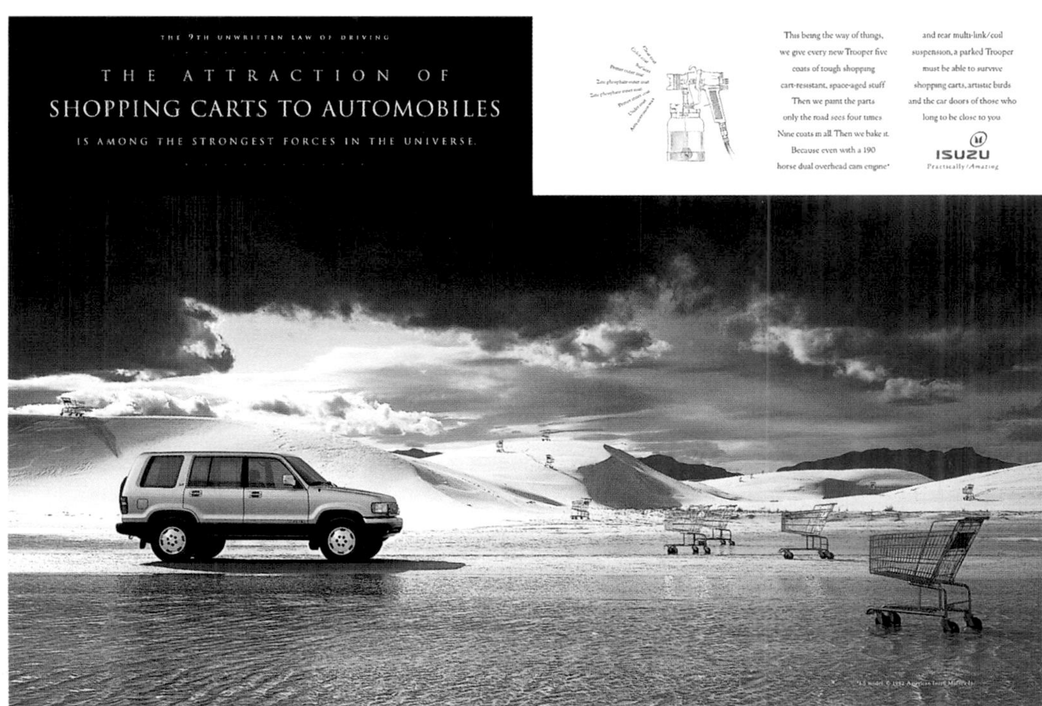

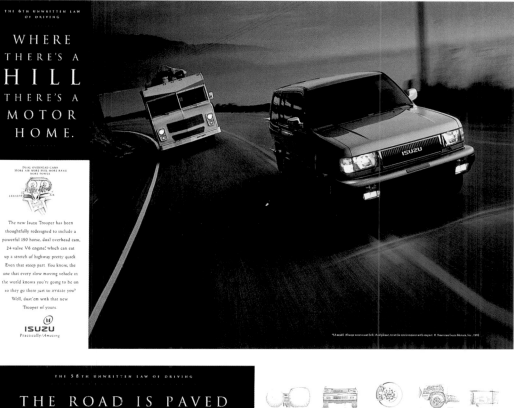

Client: American Isuzu Motors Inc. **Creative Directors:** Jeff Goodby, Rich Silverstien **Art Directors:** David Page, Erich Joiner **Copywriter:** Dave O'Hare **Photographer:** Duncan Sim

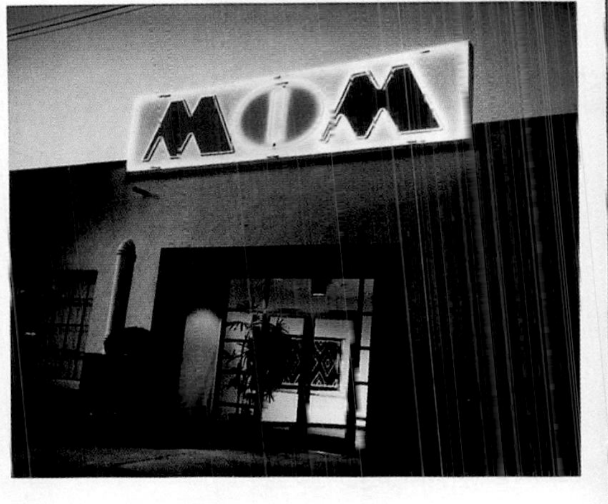

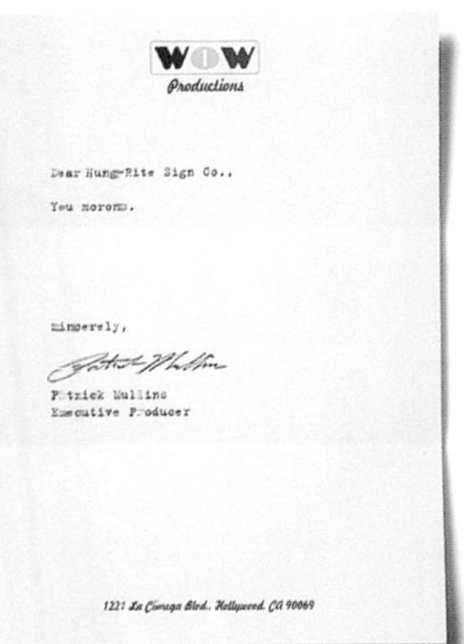

WOW
Productions

Dear Hung-Rite Sign Co.,

You morons.

Sincerely,

Patrick Mullins
Executive Producer

1221 La Cienega Blvd., Hollywood, CA 90069

Honey, you always do that.

No, I don't.

Yes you do.

No, I don't.

Wanna bet?

Look, lady:

It's not my dog.

My dog stays tied up all day.

Besides, my dog went to obedience school.

No way it's my dog.

Lots of dogs run loose in this neighborhood.

I guarantee you it's not my dog.

Dear Neighbor:

It's your dog.

2/4 2:45 pm

THE TALK OF THE TOWN
Private Drees had survived that random Scud attack on the Army barracks near Dhahran. "I caught my breath for a second and looked, and the whole building was gone," he continued. "My bunk was against the wall and it was gone. I reached back and pieces of my leg were missing. My right shoe was off. I tried to chase it around, and I couldn't.
THE NEW YORKER
WHEN YOU READ IT, YOU'LL SEE

The sorts of looks that people in the nineteenth century considered ravishing (Lillian Russell's, Lillie Langtry's) for the most part leave us indifferent today. That our taste in faces and bodies changes from one era to the next is clear; that it changes for the better, however, is not.
IN FASHION
The Eye of the Beholder
THE NEW YORKER
WHEN YOU READ IT, YOU'LL SEE

A REPORTER AT LARGE
I wasn't drunk. I wasn't impulsive. I damned well wanted a tattoo. My brother had a tattoo. Real sailors had tattoos. People tell me I'm supposed to regret it. Unless you're convinced you want it, you shouldn't do it. There ain't no turning back.
THE NEW YORKER
WHEN YOU READ IT, YOU'LL SEE

IN-LINE SKATING: Protects hand after attempted double Ore-Ida.

BOXING: Protects hand when throwing vicious left uppercut. Interestingly enough, does nothing when receiving same.

SOCCER: Protects hand from

SCUBA: Protects hand in frigid water.

SNOWBOARDING: Protects hand during big air fall and skiers

BASEBALL: Protects hand from 90mph split-finger fastball, unless ball bounces in dirt, then

RAPELLING: Protects hand from severe rope burn and unseen bird poop on ledge.

MOTORCYCLE: Protects hand

ICE HOCKEY: Protects hand from high velocity puck. Has tendency to come off during fights.

CRICKET: Protects hand

LACROSSE: Protects hand from stick-wielding opponent hell-bent on putting small ball in net.

CYCLING GLOVES: Until now, they've been pretty useless fashion statements. So to appreciate the new Body Geometry glove, hold your left hand palm side up. See that fleshy area on the right side just above your wrist? There's a nerve that runs through there called the ulnar nerve that, when it's compressed, can make your hand go numb. Ever have that happen on a long ride? Check out your current glove. Is there enough padding? Is it correctly placed? Do you even know? Hence the Body Geometry's purposefulness. It's the only anatomically correct glove designed specifically to protect the ulnar nerve in both hands. To keep you riding longer and in more comfort. And—well, yeah okay, they look pretty good too.

specialized.com

INNOVATE OR DIE

Tough as nails? Oh come on, you'll have to do better than that.

You'd have to want to pop an Armadillo tire. And even then you probably can't. Thanks to our proprietary casing and DuPont KEVLAR,® Armadillos deflect incoming particles and significantly prevent punctures and side cuts, making them virtually indestructible. Centuries? Double centuries? Try millenniums. One guy reports riding four thousand miles on a set of Armadillos without a single flat. Can this possibly be true? Well according to an independent test, Armadillos are far and away the toughest tires out there. And yet the smoothness of the ride is never compromised, which is the whole point. Or points, as it were.

Mountain

Hybrid

Road

specialized.com

INNOVATE OR DIE

Cheat the wind, play larceny with time, expose your friends as the pathetic climbers that they are.

From its aerodynamic thinwall tubes to its European road racing geometry, the M4 is the personification of speed. Its tubeset componentry reads like the Periodic Table of Elements: magnesium, aluminum, copper, silicon and vanadium, further complemented by Mavic, ITT, Dura-Ace and Time. Lighter, stiffer, stronger, the M4 climbs, descends, corners and sprints like a true custom. And according to an independent test in the NASA wind tunnel, it does so with an exceedingly low coefficient of drag. Now that the M4 has finally hit American roads—well it's worth checking out, even if only to hear those guys sucking wind behind you.

specialized.com

INNOVATE OR DIE

Client: Hewlett-Packard **Creative Director:** Steve Simpson **Art Directors:** Todd Grant, Keith Anderson **Copywriter:** Michael McKay **Account Executive:** Amber Adoue **Photographer:** Kelvin Hudson

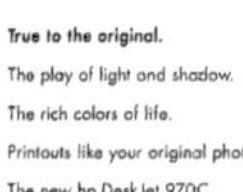

True to the original.
The play of light and shadow.
The rich colors of life.
Printouts like your original photos.
The new hp DeskJet 970C.

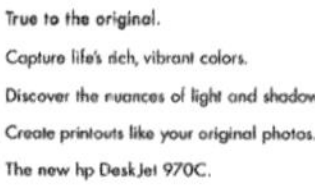

True to the original.
Capture life's rich, vibrant colors.
Discover the nuances of light and shadow.
Create printouts like your original photos.
The new hp DeskJet 970C.

True to the original.

Discover life's vibrant colors.

Capture delicate detail and rich shadow.

Printouts that are most like your original photos.

The new hp DeskJet 970C.

Invent, create and inspire for just $399*.

hp.com/go/original.

Civilization Is Advancing At A Stately 18 Knots.

Long before reaching your destination, you will experience a sense of having arrived. Such is life aboard our newest ship, the intimate *Royal Viking Queen*, and her larger, more stately companion, the elegant *Royal Viking Sun*.

Here, all that has made sailing Royal Viking Line so wondrous over the years is heightened as never before. Consider mingling with learned experts in World Affairs. Or collecting secrets of aquatic life from the Cousteau Society.

Elsewhere, guest chefs the likes of the renowned Paul Bocuse will provide exquisite nourishment for areas found somewhat south of the mind.

We do not wish to prod, but if this appeals to your sense of adventure, there is no better time to experience it all than now as we depart for 165 charmed ports including the storied waters of Europe. Your travel agent has particulars, or call 1 (800) 457-8599. We look forward to seeing you on board.

Royal Viking Line

If on the world you're after, send yourself our way. The five-star ships of Royal Viking Line await you, serving 145 ports on six continents with cruises 10 to 44 days in length. For a copy of our 1989 Cruise Atlas, contact your travel agent or call us at (800) 426-0821. As always, we look forward to seeing you on board.

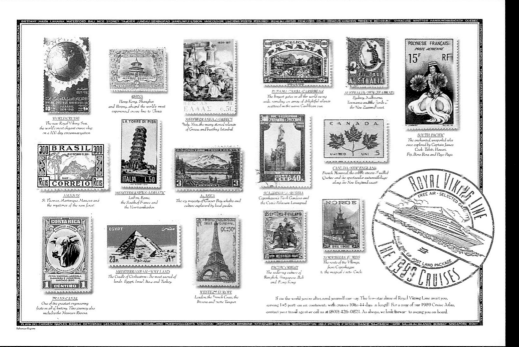

Arriving At The Proper State Of Mind Requires Just The Right Vehicle.

Pictured here: The Royal Viking Sun, Berlitz's Number One Cruise Vessel, her hold full of pleasant dreams, somewhere off the coast of Italy.

There Are No Maps To Steer You East Or West

Yet it is possible to get there, and perhaps the best way is by ship.

But not just any ship. It should be one filled with the elegance and little touches that make a vessel worthy of being designated five-star-plus. We have not just one, but an entire fleet of such remarkable crafts.

Each of our ships is equipped with amiable dining rooms that offer unhurried single seating. Aboard every one, you'll find kitchens where 33 European-trained chefs will prepare fine delicacies. In the staterooms, fresh flowers appear magically each morning. Surrounding each vessel are the most spacious, most strollable decks.

At every turn, you'll witness the alert, gracious service that inspired the readers of *Travel-Holiday* magazine to vote us the Most Courteous Cruise Line for three years running.

So in the end, it is not a question of whether you can arrive at the proper state of mind by way of our ships. It is merely a question of how soon you will choose to do so. Your travel agent will help you decide, or call us at (800) 426-0821. We look forward to your call and to seeing you on board.

An anchor from Norway, deck chair seating on authentic Burmese teak. These are the kind of touches you'll find — and will be provided.

Client: Royal Viking Line **Creative Directors:** Jeffrey Goodby, Rich Silverstein **Art Directors:** (top) Rich Silverstein (middle and bottom) Betsy Zimmerman **Photographers:** (top) Nadav Kander (bottom) Harvey Lloyd

Gas. Food. Lodging. (Last two optional.)

Presenting the Boxster. In seconds, the top glides back and lets in the world. The 200 horsepower, mid-mounted flat six then leaves everything else behind. Including any primitive urges involving sustenance or shelter.

Starting at $39,980. Contact us at 1-800-Porsche or http://www.porsche.com and understand the statement:

Porsche. There is no substitute.™

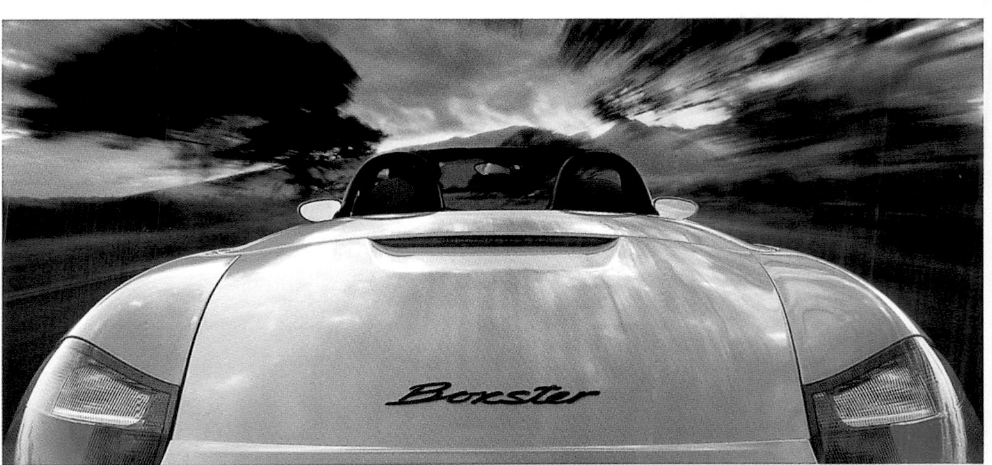

1956 meets 2001.

Presenting the Boxster. It's classic, yet futuristic. It's a cross between a 550 Spyder and the space shuttle.

It's the first mid-engine Porsche roadster in over 40 years. And it's in the Here and Now.

Starting at $39,980. Contact us at 1-800-PORSCHE or http://www.porsche.com and come to believe:

Porsche. There is no substitute.™

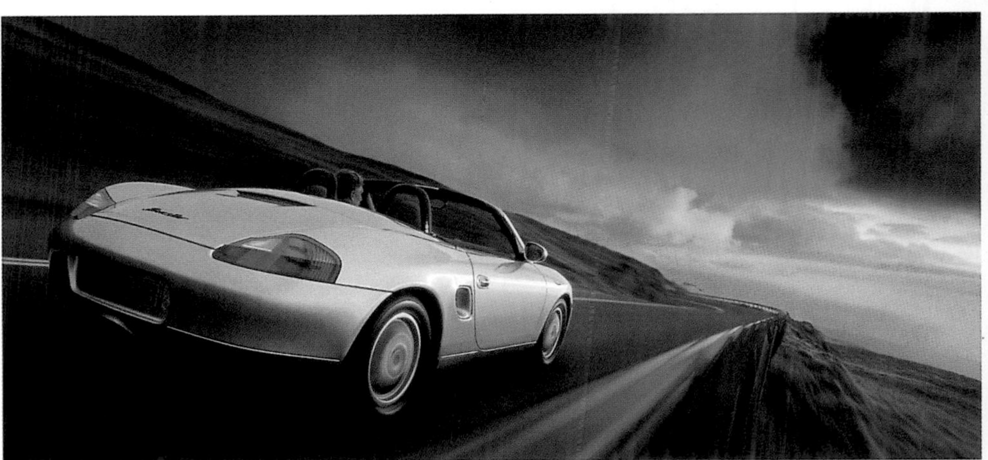

Bring a map.

Presenting the Boxster. The top disappears in seconds. Thanks to the mid-mounted flat six, so do you. But not to worry, you can always use the two trunks for survival gear.

Starting at $39,980. Contact us at 1-800-Porsche or http://www.porsche.com and realize:

Porsche. There is no substitute.™

got milk?

got milk?

Got
Milk?

got milk?

Client: California Fluid Milk Advisory Board **Creative Directors:** Jeff Goodby, Rich Silverstein **Art Director:** Sean Ehringer **Copywriter:** Harry Cocciolo **Photographer:** Holly Stewart

Page 62 *Sonicare* (left) Note to dentist: Brush! (right) Has a patient of yours ever gotten so excited? Getting people to do something no one cares about or enjoys is always a challenge. One solution is to have chubby guys appear with their shirts off.

Page 63 *Nike* Nike had perennially advertised the functionality of their sports apparel, insisting that if the clothes worked well, they would look good. This campaign turned that dynamic on its head, unabashedly suggesting that if the clothes looked this good, they must work. We made this point by putting these high-tech garments on some pretty fine looking young athletes. Long after we left the account, this campaign still runs.

Page 64-65 *Beaver Creek* Creek Beaver Creek is one of the most beautiful and exclusive mountain resorts in North America, drawing its inspiration from the famed Chamonix. We wanted to add a patina of time and tradition to this rather new resort (new money may be new, but who likes to be reminded of that?). To do this, we resurrected a classic European ski poster style, selling the specific contemporary benefits of the resort, but wrapping in a feeling of timelessness.

Page 66 *Isuzu* It's a fact that very few SUV's are ever taken off-road or even put into four-wheel drive. This was certainly true of Isuzu's higher priced entry, the Trooper. We knew that Trooper owners rarely went looking for risky adventures, but wanted assurance that, if adventure unexpectedly came to them, they'd be prepared. These surreal ads did just that, simply and beautifully.

Page 67 *Polaroid* Polaroid had traditionally advertised their cameras in a way that suggested they could compete with the image and archival quality of 35 millimeter film. This was poppycock. No one took important pictures with a Polaroid. In the advertising, we tried to remind people of the way they really did use Polaroid film—as a form of instant evidence, as a record, or as a fun conversation piece. A Polaroid picture, we suggested, was not a passive thing. It was a catalyst that could make something happen right now.

Page 68 *The New Yorker* It was hard to get media planners to recommend The New Yorker to their clients because the planners themselves rarely read it. Usually, in fact, they thought of it as a ponderous, wordy pile of greyness with no visual interest whatsoever. In the ads, we excerpted a short, provocative piece of writing ("short" is the key word here) and paired it with the kind of big splashy visual that, yeah, never really appeared in the magazine. But the combination suddenly made planners see a spark, a youthfulness, and a relevancy they hadn't thought was there.

Page 69 *Specialized Bicycle Components, Inc.* As the bicycling market became more and more sophisticated, Specialized needed to seize and maintain a feeling of technological leadership. These ads were a big handful of technological developments exclusive to the brand, thrown into the face of placid consumers skimming vertical bike publications. Nothing else in bike-land looked like these ads.

Page 70 *Hewlett-Packard* In the color printer marketplace, HP's competitors had touted the number of ink dots per square inch as a way of measuring the effectiveness of a printer. HP engineers told us there was much more to it than that, arguing that dot patterns and sizes in the HP system added up to imagery that was simply much more true to the original. We demonstrated this more straightforward claim in magazines and outdoor advertising by slicing out slabs of colorful stuff and showing them emanating from the printer. It was unforgettable imagery, coinciding with a sharp spike in HP sales.

Page 71 *Royal Viking Line* RVL was perhaps the first nationally-recognized magazine campaign we ever did, and certainly one of the most copied. We retooled a typeface to make it distinctively our own; invented the unique border with RVL's destinations on it; and, in the gleaming layouts, tried to evoke the whiteness of the ships. In our first comps, we had no images of the vessels, thinking that was so, well, obvious. The client and focus groups, however, told us emphatically otherwise. After that, Duncan Simms, Nadav Kander, Jay Maisel and Harvey Lloyd took long, grueling trips to the Caribbean every year for these glorious shots.

Page 72 *Porsche* For many years, Porsche had inexplicably photographed their cars at rest on nice grey stages. Clint Clemons put the car in motion and gave it an unearthly beauty with these streaky backgrounds. Around these images, we tried to create the most graphic copy ads ever. Our writers competed to make the headlines shorter and shorter (there was a five word limit at one point), because the Franklin Gothic looked so good when it got big and fat. This campaign won the magazine publishers' highest award, the Kelly, that carried with it a cash prize of 100,000 smackers.

Page 73 *California Fluid Milk Advisory Board* How many other campaigns have been able to compress headline, tagline, product name, and brand positioning into two words? This work reversed a twenty-year decline in milk consumption by dropping the tired strategy that milk was good for you and adopting instead an approach that said: If you've got a brownie, you're going to need some milk. And if you don't have it, you're going to be really really screwed. The campaign was originally developed just for California, but soon other milk boards across the country—and even the national board—began paying to use it themselves. The thing has spawned a whole industry of t-shirts, mugs, and plastic cows.

700 California Street San Francisco, California 94108 tel. 415-392-0669 fax. 415-788-4303

GSD&M

VISIONARY IDEAS THAT MAKE A DIFFERENCE

GSD&M

GSD&M was founded by six University of Texas graduates in 1971, based on the premise that big ideas generate big results. Over the years we have grown from college kids with "big ideas" to a nationally acclaimed agency that bills more than a billion dollars per year. Now "home" to more than 700 people, we still embrace the entrepreneurial spirit that fueled our growth. ■ Our creative mission statement summarizes our philosophy on producing great work. We use this as the guiding principle in producing ideas that help to build our clients' businesses: "Advertising is an

Uninvited Guest." ■ Advertising is an uninvited guest in people's homes, cars, and some of the most private moments in their lives. Therefore, we must intrigue them. Captivate them with the way we look, the things we say. We must entertain them. Encourage them to laugh (or at least smile), to cry (or at least feel empathy), and sometimes, simply to think. We must persuade them and convince them that what we have to offer is genuinely unique and valuable. Otherwise, it is unlikely we will be invited back. Successful advertising becomes an Invited Guest—the first step toward every advertiser's ultimate goal: brand loyalty.

from left to right: Steve Miller, VP Group Creative Director, Juan Perez, VP Group Creative Director, Guy Bommarito, Sr. VP Group Creative Director, Daniel Russ, Sr. VP Group Creative Director, Rich Tlapek, VP Group Creative Director, David Crawford, Sr. VP Group Creative Director, Tom Gilmore, Sr. VP Group Creative Director, Brent Ladd, Sr. VP Group Creative Director. Photo by Ellen Lampi; not pictured: Jeremy Postaer, Sr. VP Group Creative Director

Client: Land Rover **Creative Directors:** David Crawford, Jeremy Postaer **Art Directors:** Rob Story, David Crawford **Copywriters:** Michael Buss, Jeremy Postaer **Account Executives:** Nancy George, Barry Hayden **Photographer:** Dennis Fagen **Production:** Kelly G

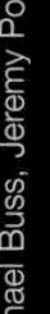

IF WE'VE LEARNED ONE THING IN 30 YEARS OF BUILDING RANGE ROVERS, IT IS THIS:

AN OSTRICH EGG WILL FEED EIGHT MEN.

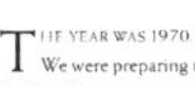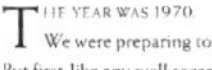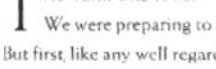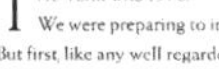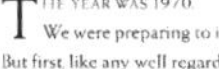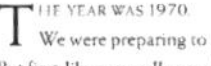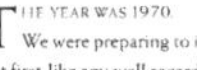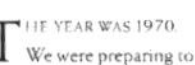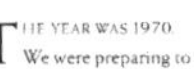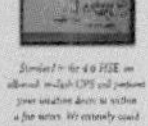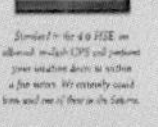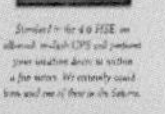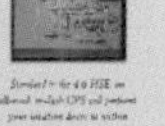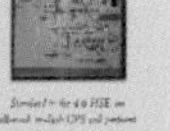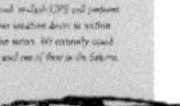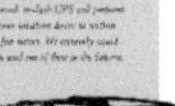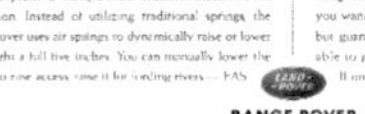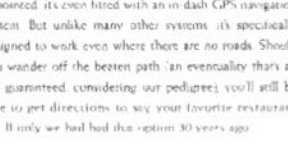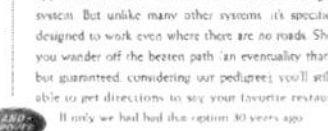

THE YEAR WAS 1970.

We were preparing to introduce our latest — and some say greatest — accomplishment to the world: the Range Rover. But first, like any well regarded car company, we tested it extensively in the field. ¶ However, unlike any other well regarded car company, when we say "tested," we mean "brutalized." And when we say "field," we mean "Sahara Desert." ¶ On that trek

2001

4.6 HSE

The very first luxury SUV.

A smooth ride is good for digestion.

What option do you have?

RANGE ROVER

HE DIDN'T SUFFER FOOLS GLADLY.

OR, FOR THAT MATTER, UNCOMFORTABLE SEATS.

RUMOR HAS IT THAT WINSTON CHURCHILL SO CHERISHED HIS TRUSTY LAND ROVER THAT HE WAS WILLING TO FORGIVE, shall we say, an unfortunate lack of proper padding. As you might imagine, that anyone, let alone Great Britain's most prolific public speaker, would suffer a sore bum while traversing in a Land Rover just didn't sit well with us. Thus began a

Life was rough before Range Rover.

Survival: the ultimate luxury.

Brutally posh.

A standing invitation to be seated.

2001

4.6 HSE

RANGE ROVER

Client: KAOS Children's Salon Art **Creative Directors:** Brent Ladd, Brian Booker **Art Director:** Brent Ladd **Copywriter:** Brian Booker **Account Executive:** Jaye Peterson **Photographer:** Dennis Fagen **Production Artist:** Heather Segrest

Client: Metropolitan Winds **Art Director:** Matt Davis **Copywriter:** Kent Portman **Photographer:** Andrew Yates

A ship doesn't
have to
SINK
to kill
THOUSANDS.
The journey from Africa to America killed more people than World War II and the Titanic combined. Visit the Museum of African American History and find out what really happened.
MUSEUM of AFRICAN AMERICAN HISTORY

How did your
ANCESTORS
come to America?
BY BOAT, BY TRAIN
or by
FORCE?
During the long trip from Africa to America the slaves were forced to live in spaces the size of coffins. And for many, these spaces became just that. Visit the Museum of African American History and find out what really happened.
MUSEUM of AFRICAN AMERICAN HISTORY

Client: Museum of African American History **Creative Director:** Brian Born **Art Director:** Lynn Sarnow **Copywriter:** Karen Schwartz **Account Executive:** Brian Born **Photographer:** Tony Pearce

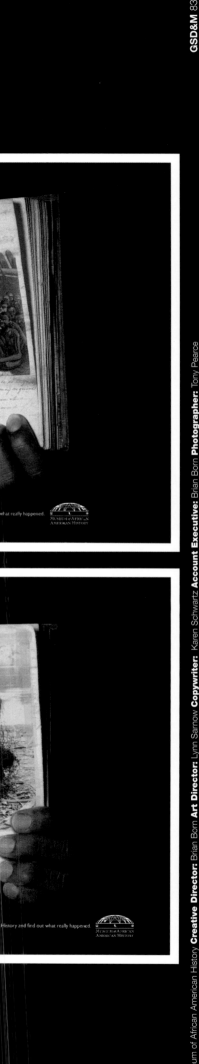

Client: Pennzoil Quaker State Corp. Creative Directors: David Crawford, Rich Tarry Art Director: Brett Stiles Copywriter: Tom Campion Photographer: R.J. Muna

People drooling over your car. It may not be pretty, but it's a problem we'd all like to have. That's why there's Classic.® It has the highest concentration of carnauba among the leading waxes. So your car gets a deep, rich shine with unparalleled protection every time. Since 1952, for a really great wax there's always been Classic.

CLASSIC NOT ONLY GIVES YOUR CAR A DEEP, RICH SHINE, IT ALSO PROTECTS AGAINST UNSIGHTLY DROOL.

LOVE. HONOR. POLISH.™

See, it works out for everyone. You get a great-looking car. And your wife gets you. All because Classic® Quick Wax™ with carnauba is such a quick and easy way to give your car a deep, rich shine with unparalleled protection. Since 1952, for a really great wax there's always been Classic.

WITH QUICK WAX, YOU'LL SPEND LESS TIME WITH THE ONE YOU LOVE. BUT IT DOES FREE UP TIME FOR YOUR WIFE.

Classic

LOVE. HONOR. POLISH.™

Client: Shred Doc Office Shredding Machines **Creative & Art Director:** Brent Ladd **Copywriter:** Rich Tlapek **Photographer:** Peter Rad **Digital Retoucher:** Michele Hoelscher **Production Artist:** Heather Segrest

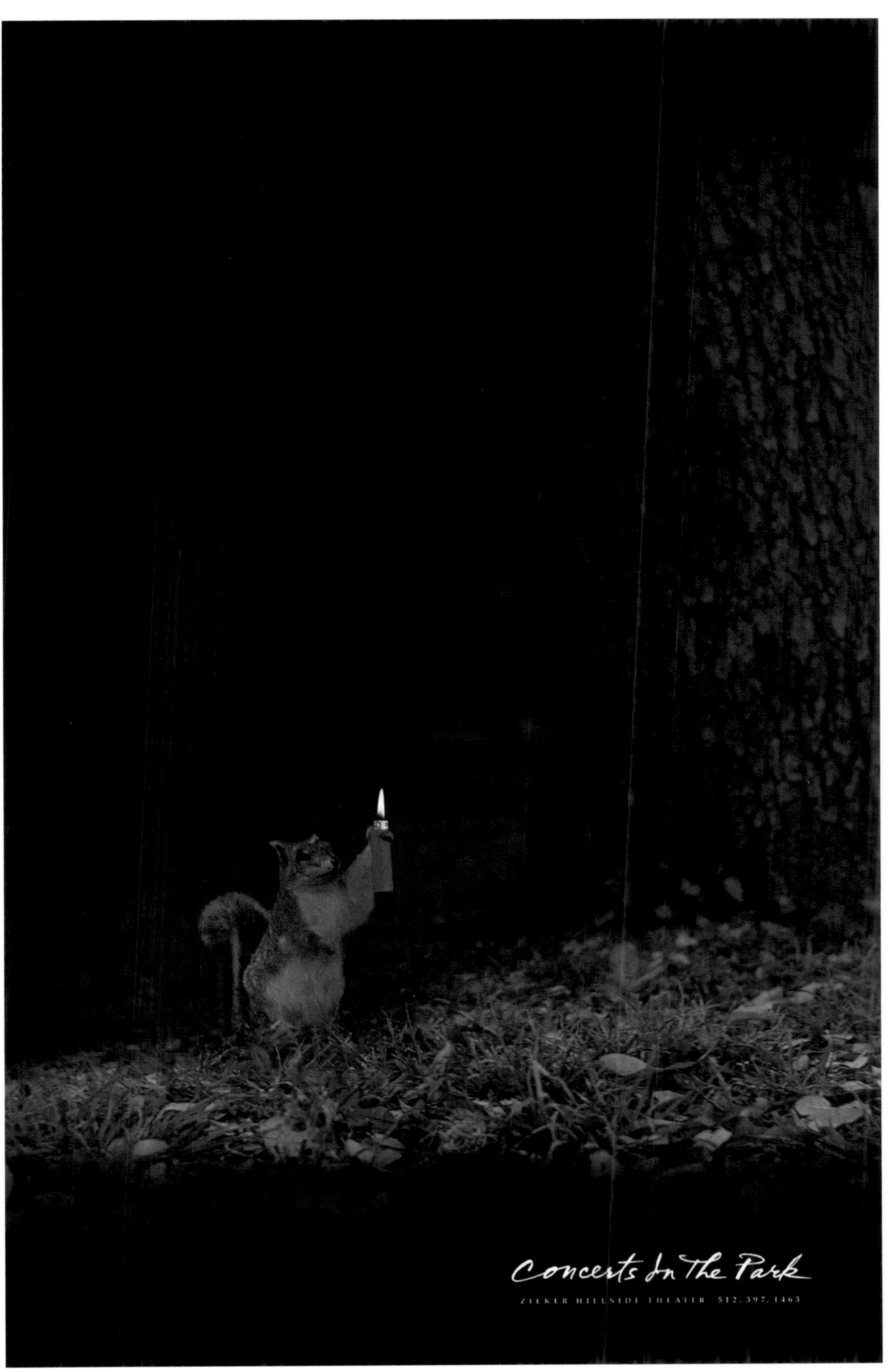

Client: Zilkor Park **Creative Director:** Rich Tlapek **Art Director, Copywriter and Account Executive:** Brian Born

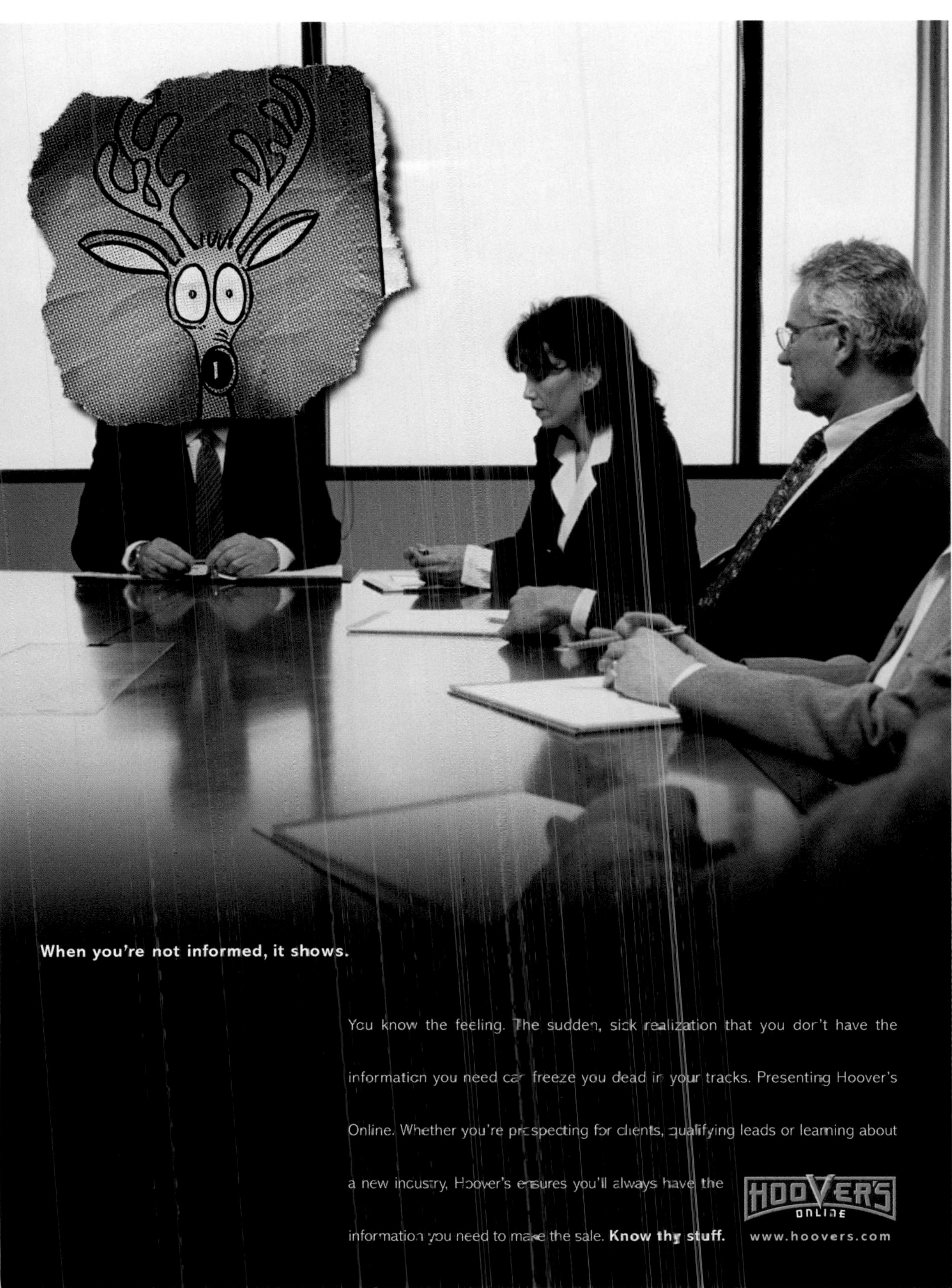

When you're not informed, it shows.
You know the feeling. The sudden, sick realization that you don't have the information you need can freeze you dead in your tracks. Presenting Hoover's Online. Whether you're prospecting for clients, qualifying leads or learning about a new industry, Hoover's ensures you'll always have the information you need to make the sale. **Know thy stuff.**
HOOVER'S ONLINE
www.hoovers.com

Client: Hoover's Online **Creative Directors:** Cameron Day, David Crawford **Art Director:** Rob Story **Copywriter:** Michael Buss **Account Executives:** Steve Dalbey, Christine Cook, Kyle Woolsey, Christy Casey **Illustrators:** Kevin Peake, Mike Peters

ous **Creative Directors:** Karen Gregory, Don Wade **Art Director:** Jocus Felix **Copywriter:** Clint Carter **Account Executive:** Kristin Schell **Photographer:** Bill Debold

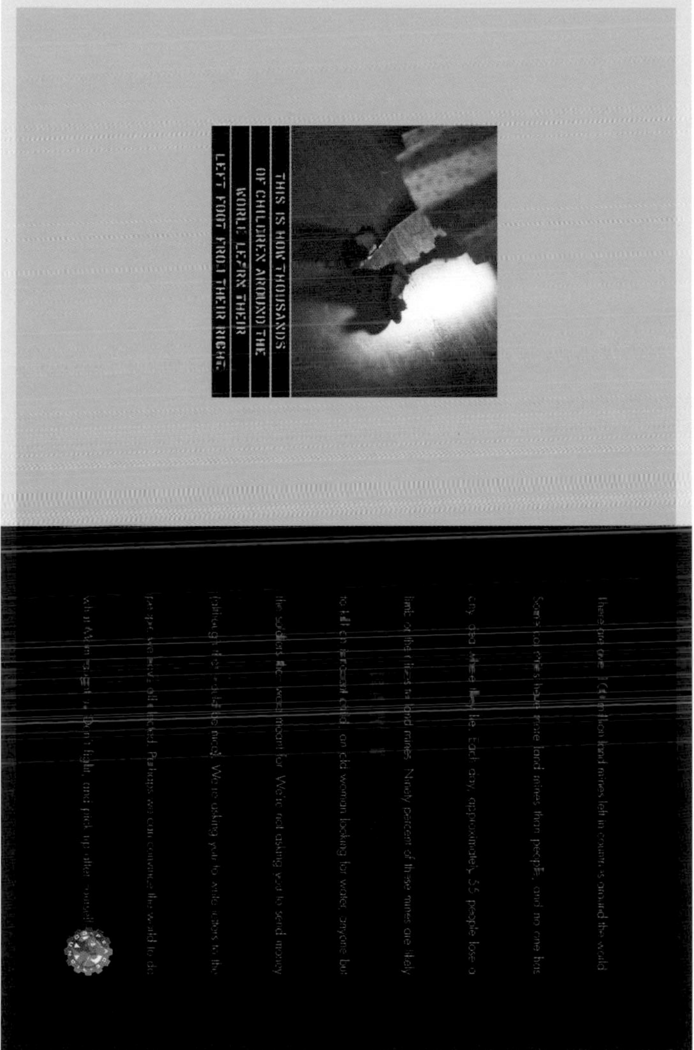

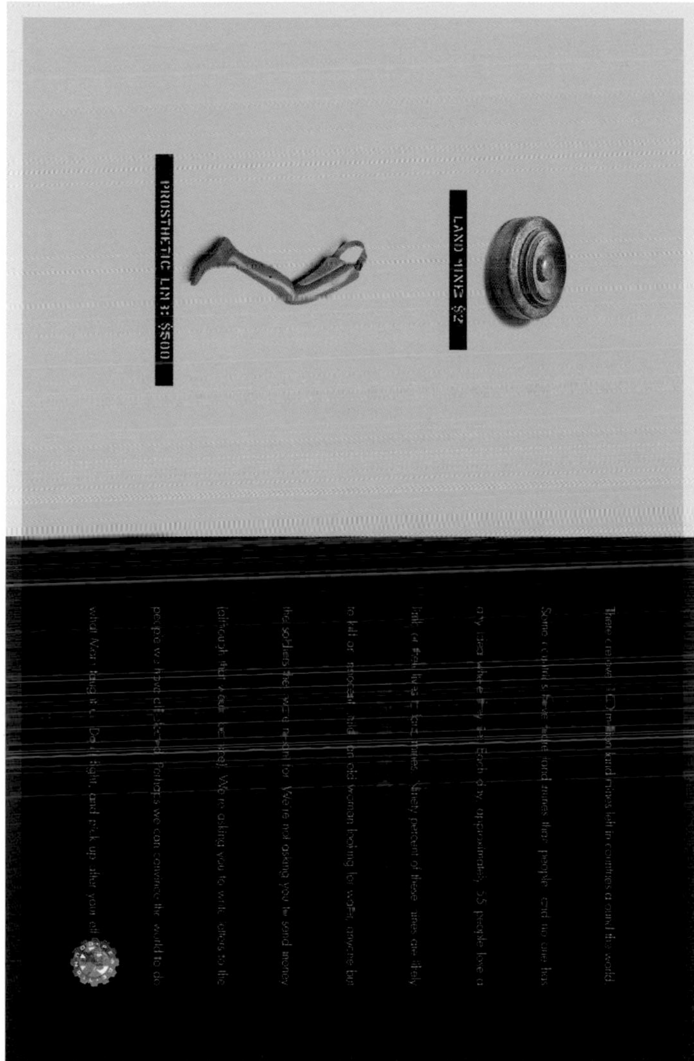

Client: Peace Council **Creative Directors:** Brent Ladd, Daniel Russ **Art Director and Designer:** Brent Ladd **Copywriter:** Daniel Russ **Photographers:** Brad Guice, Jimmy Williams **Production Artist:** Anne Rix

Page 78 *Land Rover* Land Rover's Range Rover vehicle was introduced to North America in 1987, but we found that consumers still didn't really know what the Land Rover company was all about. They have a great story to tell. One that no other car company can claim. This campaign tells that story.

Page 79 *Southwest Airlines* A simple visual conveys that Southwest Airlines is proud to be a sponsor of the arts.

Page 80 *Larry Mahan* This ad was created to promote a new high-end cowboy boot designed and worn by Larry Mahan.

Page 81 *KAOS* These striking in-store posters bring together the mischevious nature of kids and hair salon icons to represent chaos. The tag line reads, "A salon for kids of all ages." The KAOS logo is made of small "hair-like" lines. The client wanted work that would stand out and position KAOS as a hair salon that specializes in children's haircuts.

Page 82 *Metropolitan Winds* We needed to build awareness for a concert series by the Metropolitan Winds of Dallas that would feature the music of film composer John Williams. We decided to capitalize on the near universal recognition some of his films already had by combining a conductor with the image most associated with each movie (i.e. light saber). The results were overwhelming. The concerts attained record ticket sales, performing to near sell-out audiences.

Page 83 *The Museum of African American History* These provocative ads spark human interest in The Museum of African American History.

Page 84 *Pennzoil Quaker State Corp.* Classic is a special wax. While it may not be well known to owners of Yugos, people who take pride in their cars have heard of it. We targeted these ads to people who have a special relationship with their car and in many cases, have special cars. It's a bond that's more sacred to some than marriage. We're helping them not to screw it up.

Page 85 *Shred Doc* Here is a document shredder. It is not an ordinary piece of office equipment, as such, you might not think you need it. This campaign uses the latest scandals, political and otherwise in a humorous way to remind you about how, in the wrong hands, a simple document can make life difficult for you.

Page 86 *Zilker Park* Zilker concerts are enjoyed by everyone in the park.

Page 87 *Hoover's Online* Everyone wants to be successful. In business, the difference between success and abject, spectacular failure can sometimes be as simple as a piece of information. If only there were a single place where you could go to find business information. Then you'd have something.

Page 88 *Parents Anonymous* This ad aims to inform people about an upcoming prison auction.

Page 89 *Peace Council* Our goal was to raise awareness of land mines left behind after wars around the world. And the destruction to people and property that results.

828 West 6th Street Austin, Texas 78703 tel: 512-427-4928 fax: 512-427-7928

KesselsKramer

KesselsKramer

KesselsKramer works out of a church built in 1877, which now contains a wooden fort, a golden beach tower, a porcelain dog, the head of Lenin (damaged) and the occasional group of touring nuns. The agency, set up just over five years ago by Erik Kessels and Johan Kramer, is a collective of 25+ people of all nationalities—coming from places as far afield as the USA, Sweden, Turkey, China, Germany and the UK. The group is based in Amsterdam, the Netherlands, but enjoys work on both a national and international level for clients like Ben, Hans Brinker Budget Hotel, Australian, Heineken, Levi's, Bertelsmann, Audi, Novib/Oxfam, *Het Parool* newspaper, U2, Turkcell, Bols and *TIME*. The philosophy is based on a desire to get involved with not just advertising, but the whole marketing process (including parts of the marketing process that haven't yet been invented), and to dig deep into the brand, turning it inside out and upside down. This could transpire into finding a new name for a brand, or a new house style and attitude, as well as developing the brand and helping it grow and evolve. It could also involve helping the brand develop into new areas, meaning anything from product design to creating a long-term future

strategy. To achieve this, KesselsKramer works with a strong team in strategy and creation and also has the added advantage of an in-house tv-production company. This enables the agency to direct a lot of its own tv commercials, music videos (for Tom Waits, for example), short films, documentaries, etc. KesselsKramer also oversees the progress of a new kind of ever-changing brand called "do" (www.dosurf.com), which has seen itself turn into everything from innovative household products (do create) to a 24-hour worldwide internet conference about television (do-tv). Very shortly, the agency plans to open a new business unit to oversee trends and developments in idea hacking—something set to overturn the whole communications industry in the next few years. ■ Just a few thoughts about the working process coming out of the church: There shouldn't really be a boundary between disciplines. This means you can work on everything from album covers, print ads and websites to video clips, book design and shopping bags. Clients shouldn't really be clients; they should be people you enjoy meeting and working with. Inspire those around you and be inspired by them. Be humble. Be aware outside of advertising. Walk with open eyes. Gnomes can talk if you ask them the right questions.

Erik Kessels (left) and Johan Kramer (right)

Client: Ascrum Rugby **Creative Directors:** Erik Kessels, Johan Kramer **Art Director:** Karen Heuter **Copywriters:** David Bell, Tyler Whisnand **Photographer:** Audrey van Aarssen

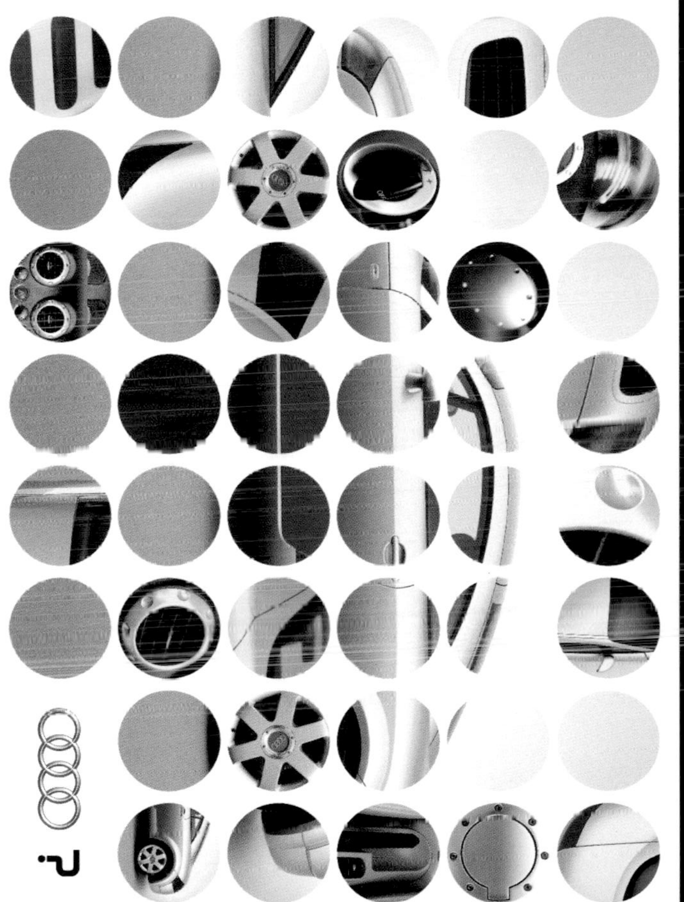

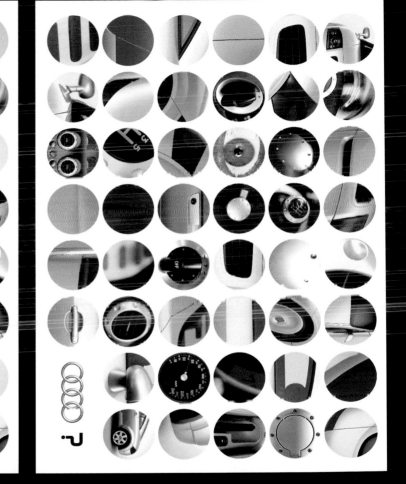

Client: Audi **Creative Directors:** Erik Kessels, Johan Kramer **Art Director:** Erik Kessels **Copywriter:** Johan Kramer **Account Executive:** Darren Brady-Harris **Photographer:** Gerd-Jan van der Lugt **Strategy:** Matthijs de Jongh

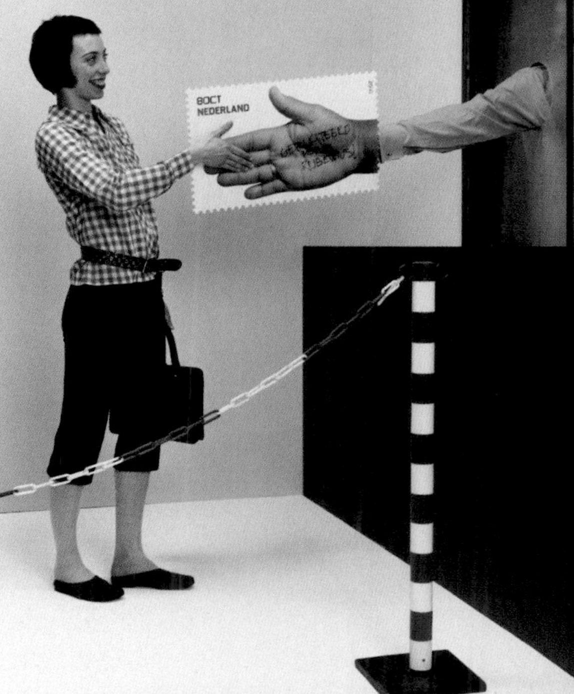

Client: PTT Post **Creative Directors:** Erik Kessels, Johan Kramer **Art Director:** Erik Kessels **Copywriter:** Johan Kramer **Photographer:** Lies Musch

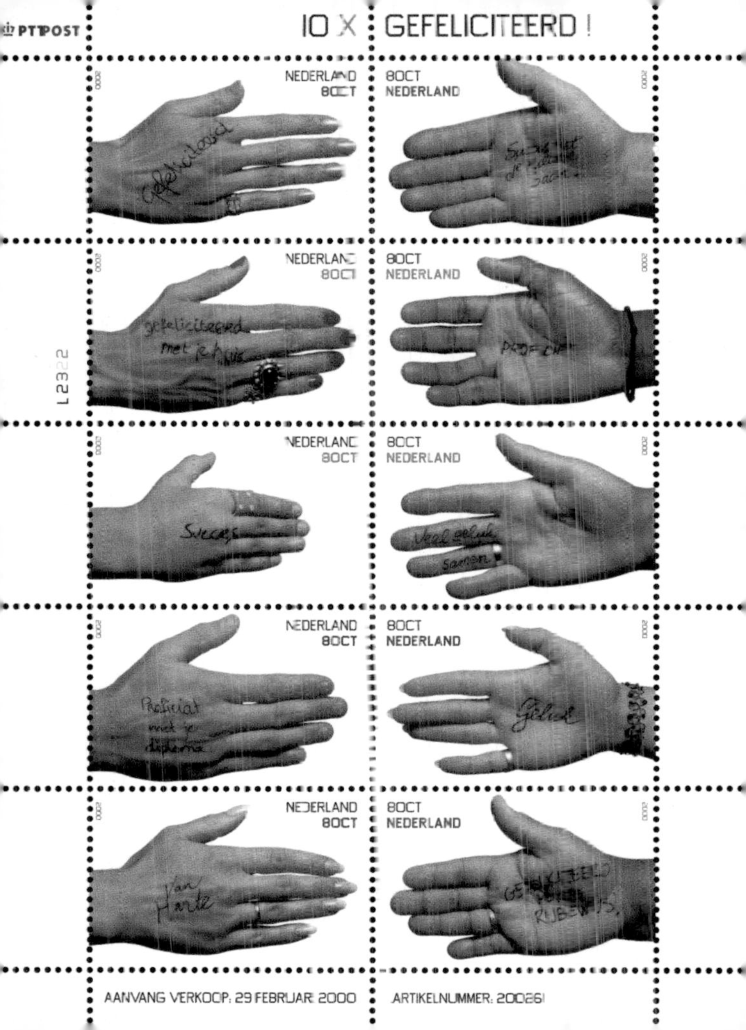
PTTPOST
10 X GEFELICITEERD !
NEDERLAND 80CT
80CT NEDERLAND
NEDERLAND 80CT
80CT NEDERLAND
L2322
NEDERLAND 80CT
80CT NEDERLAND
NEDERLAND 80CT
80CT NEDERLAND
NEDERLAND 80CT
80CT NEDERLAND
AANVANG VERKOOP: 29 FEBRUARI 2000
ARTIKELNUMMER: 200261

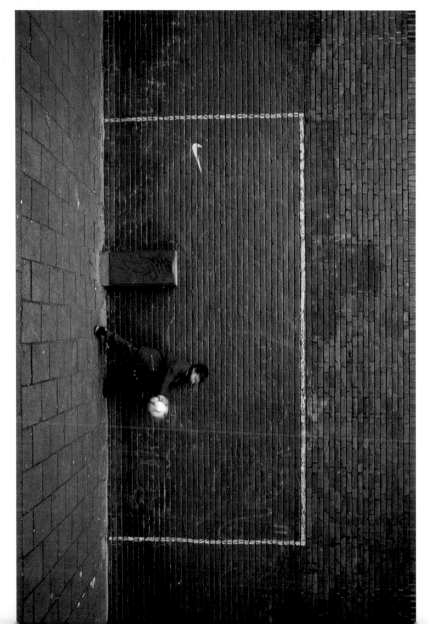

Client: Nike **Creative Directors:** Erik Kessels, Johan Kramer **Art Director:** Erik Kessels **Copywriter:** Johan Kramer **Photographer:** Jaap Stahlie

Naar Sydney
op de Ben* manier
Naar Sydney
op de Ben* manier
Zorg dat je de Ben* Olympische mobiele telefoon in je bezit krijgt.
Voor f 149,- heb je de nieuwe Samsung SGH 2100 met Olympisch design. Doe mee aan de prijsvraag en wacht op een SMS bericht van Ben*. Heb je een SMS ontvangen? Gefeliciteerd, je hebt gratis kaartjes voor het bijwonen van de Olympische Spelen in Sydney gewonnen.
Wil je meer weten over de Ben* Olympische mobiele telefoon en hoe je de reis- en verblijfkosten vergoed krijgt, lees dan de Ben* folder in dit tijdschrift. Veel geluk van Ben*.
Bel voor meer informatie:
0115 - 64 04 99
Ben*
Naar Sydney
op de Ben* manier
Ben*
O'NEILL
BIKES
BE ONE
BIORACER
TECHNICAL WEAR
SHIMANO
Rigida
MICHELIN
BE ONE
BIKES

Client: Nike Europe **Creative Directors:** Erik Kessels, Johan Kramer **Art Director:** Erik Kessels **Copywriters:** Johan Kramer, Tyler Whisnand **Illustrator:** Bill Mayer **Strategy:** Matthijs de Jongh

Client: Levi's Europe **Creative Directors:** Erik Kessels, Johan Kramer **Art Director:** Karen Heuter **Copywriter:** David Bell **Photographer:** Erwin Olaf **Strategy:** Matthijs de Jongh

Client: Ben **Creative Director:** Erik Kessels, Johan Kramer **Art Director:** Erik Kessels **Copywriter:** Johan Kramer **Photographer:** Bert Teunissen **Strategy:** Matthijs de Jongh

ik ben Ben®
een nieuw mobiel netwerk

ik ben Ben®
een nieuw mobiel netwerk

Het PAROOL
Beatrix Pruijt
leest Het Parool.
Abonnee sinds januari '68

Het PAROOL
Beatrix Toff
leest Het Parool.
Abonnee sinds mei '84

Het PAROOL
IONEL
BUCATARU
UIT ZEEBURG
leest Het Parool.

Het PAROOL
AYSEL
BODUR
UIT SLOTEN
leest Het Parool.

Client: Het Parool **Creative Directors:** Erik Kessels, Johan Kramer

Art Directors: (top) Erik Kessels (bottom) Erik Kessels, Harmine Louwe **Copywriters:** (top) Johan Kramer (bottom) Johan Kramer, Franklin Neuteboom **Photographer:** (top) Celine van Balen (bottom) Hans van der Meer **Strategy:** Matthijs de Jongh

Beste Audi S3-rijders,
hierboven treft u wat zwakke plekken op de Nederlandse wegen aan.
Verder zien we geen problemen.
De Audi S3
Audi
Beste Audi rijders,
we kunnen u mededelen dat 20 november onze nieuwe Roadster zal arriveren.
Bij deze bent u uitgenodigd voor een proefrit.
Audi TT Roadster
Audi

Kessels, Johan Kramer **Art Director:** Erik Kessels **Copywriter:** Johan Kramer **Photographer:** Jaap Stahlie **Strategy:** Matthijs de Jongh

WANTED
FLEA EXTERMI
NATOR
OR be a Music
Festival Roadie.
Get the Levi's Summer JobZine at the Original Levi's Store.

WANTED
FLOWER PSYCHIA
TRIST
MUST BE ABLE TO THINK AND FEEL LIKE A PLANT.
APPLY TO
BOX NO.983
OR be a Music
Festival Roadie.
Get the Levi's Summer JobZine at the Original Levi's Store.
Levi's

Erik Kessels, Johan Kramer **Art Director:** Karen Heuter **Copywriters:** David Bell, Tyler Whisnand **Photographer:** Herman Poppelaars **Production Artist:** Mark Burke **Strategy:**

Page 94 *Ascrum Rugby* Ascrum is the major rugby club in Amsterdam. To promote their home-games, we used some shock therapy to wake up some possible visitors.
Page 95 *Audi* Audi came out with a great sportscar that didn't look like an Audi. To play with this assumption, we did 3 double page newspaper ads over 3 days. Each day, we showed more and more of the whole car, but never admitted it was an Audi. Is it?
Page 96-97 *PTT Post* The Dutch Postal Service (PTT) asked us to design 10 different congratulatory stamps. With such a small size to work from, simplicity overruled the winning design: the universal icon of a hand in the hand-shaking position. Written on the hand were different messages of congratulations. Two stamps together on one letter tell a story.
Page 98 *Nike* Sometimes you don't need a lot of money, just a piece of chalk. These inner city brick walls in different European cities were changed into football goals by the simplest means possible—a service provided by Nike, friend of football.
Page 99 *Ben* To announce an offer from Ben (a new mobile network in The Netherlands and sponsor of the Dutch Olympic team) to win a trip to Sydney, ads were made with Olympic athletes shown in very proud stances. Next to them, in the same proud position, you see an ordinary person. You could choose to go to Sydney the hard way, by being an athlete, or the Ben way, which was winning a holiday to Australia.
Page 100 *Nike Europe* The future of cycling as seen through the eyes of Nike, sponsors of Tour de France jerseys.
Page 101 *Levi's Europe* Every writer and art director in this book wants to be a pop star. But being a roadie is the closest we're ever going to get. To promote Levi's summer music festival sponsorship throughout Europe, we used embaressment as a weapon. It worked.

Page 102 *Ben* We love to be involved in a project from A-Z. When a new mobile newtork came to The Netherlands, we had the chance to come up with a name and a philosophy. Since we think brands are just like human beings, we thought it would be a great to launch a company called Ben. Ben is not only a name, but also a verb in Dutch. It means "I am." During the launch, there were 40 different posters of all kinds of people saying: "I am Ben." A mobile network for everyone in The Netherlands.
Page 103 *Het Parool* (top) In the campaign for this Dutch Newspaper, KesselsKramer uses real subscribers all the time. The birthday of Queen Beatrix is a big celebration in The Netherlands. During this week, these posters went up. Of all the subscribers, KesselsKramer found 5 women with the same name as Beatrix and turned them into Queens, just for a week. (bottom) Het Parool featured foreign people living in Amsterdam (and readers of the newspaper) to celebrate football and the multi-cultural feel of the city.
Page 104 *Audi* Ads that formed part of the brand discrimination-strategy for Audi. Although it seems rather odd to focus on drivers that have already chosen your car, the idea was that these ads would spark a bit of interest in other brand devotees, who see Audi treat their drivers with integrity. The first ad points out to A3-drivers (who like to drive fast in their cars) the roads which have some bad surfaces. the second ad is honest about the bad timing of launching a convertible sportscar: in the middle of Dutch winter.
Page 105 *Levi's Europe* Summer music festival sponsoring often means just a banner or logo. Levi's and KesselsKramer chose to instead offer a summer job—as a festival roadie. Then for the communication, they motivated European youth to apply for a job, because it's better than the crop of (slightly exaggerated) dead-end dole-office jobs you're normally presented with around that age.

Loeffler Ketchum Mountjoy

this
space
for
rent

LoefflerKetchumMountjoy

Our reputation is that of a creative shop. Over our 20-year history, we have won a disproportionate share of major creative recognition—One Show, Kelly Awards, New York Art Directors (who named us "one of the five most creative small- to mid-sized shops in America"). And Graphis just named us "one of the 10 most successful agencies in the world at getting our clients' messages out."■What people don't know about us is our strength in business and marketing planning. Our senior management, strategic planning, creative and account people are jointly responsible for crafting brand positioning and communication strategy.■The results are smart, simple solutions that unleash creative thinking across all disciplines.■Our clients tend to be outspent by their competition. And that environment is where we thrive. We must be smarter in how we integrate the brand message wherever it occurs. Traditional media. Public relations. Websites. Direct marketing. Collateral, trade show and retail point-of-purchase. Employee and trade communications. Our challenge is to leverage and maximize budgets.■The quick facts: $34 million and 49 people...clients are: Mannington Floors (number two in market share to Armstrong in vinyl, second in wood flooring to Bruce, and third in the laminate category—which Pergo developed); North Carolina Travel and Tourism (grown from $6 billion to $12 billion in revenues over the 10 years we've had the account); Cargill Dow LLC (a new joint venture of Cargill and Dow Chemicals manufacturing natural-based polymers); Peachtree Doors & Windows (fighting Andersen and Pella); VELUX Skylights (also fighting the window industry); and *The Charlotte Observer* (which, as most local papers, is struggling to retain a strong position in today's media environment).■We bring years of senior-level experience in travel and tourism, banking, housing and home furnishings, sporting goods, business-to-business, and retail.■Who do we want as clients? It's very tempting to fall into the trap of growing too fast, taking on too much work, or worse, the wrong kind of work. We've chosen to work for national or major regional clients who share the same passion, the same values, as we do...who are smart and aggressive...understand the inseparable connection between smart strategy and bright, effective creative...and who want an agency relationship that is on a senior level as well as deep through both organizations.

pictured from left to right: Curtis Smith, Doug Pedersen, Ed Jones, Jim Mountjoy

Scorer's Initials ______________________________

Competitor's Signature ______________________________

Rangemaster's Signature ______________________________

Entry # ______

Range # ______

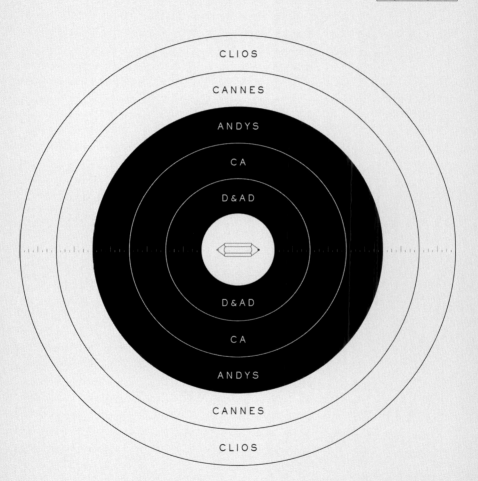

	Number of Ads	Award Value
Print		
Radio		
TV		
Internet		
Outdoor		
TOTALS		

CLIOS

CANNES

ANDYS

CA

D&AD

D&AD

CA

ANDYS

CANNES

CLIOS

THE ONE SHOW

2001 CALL FOR ENTRIES

212-979-1900 www.oneclub.com

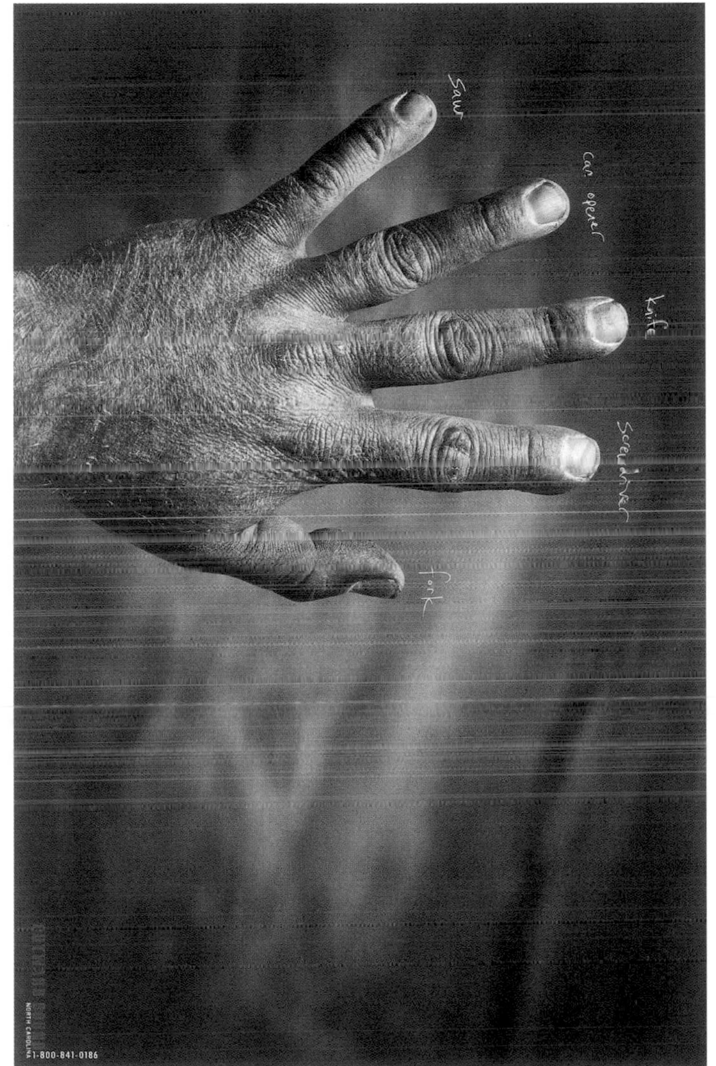

Client: Outward Bound **Creative Directors:** Jim Mountjoy, Ed Jones **Art Director:** Doug Pedersen **Copywriters:** Curtis Smith, Mike Duckworth **Account Executive:** John Ketchum **Photographer:** Jim Arndt

Some see dragons.
Some see islands.
What do you see?

It traveled millions of miles to get here.
The least you can do is let it in.
skylights and roof windows
VELUX®

Some people add square feet to their house.
Others, square miles.
skylights and roof windows
VELUX®

It was a dark and stormy night.
Cool.
skylights and roof windows
VELUX®

Client: VELUX-America Inc. **Creative Director:** Jim Mountjoy **Copywriter:** Curtis Smith **Account Executive:** Taylor Busby

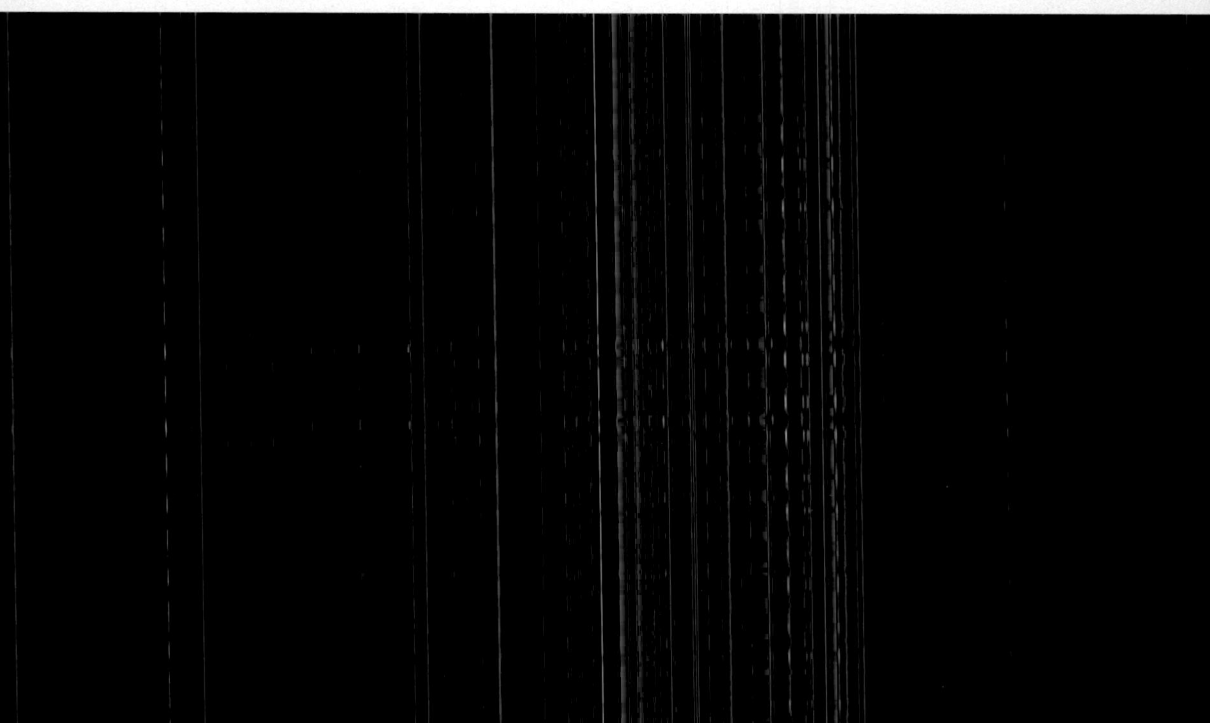
Presenting a remarkable new addition to our vinyl flooring collection: ceramic patterns with a look and feel so realistic, they've even got some very discerning experts fooled. Call 1-800-Floor-Us to find out more.
MANNINGTON

Hey,
at least the
data's safe.
Verbatim tapes, optical and floppy disks. Your best defense against data loss.

Cheer up Mac.
Remember, our data's
stored on Verbatim.
MAC'S
FIREWORKS
AL'S MATCHES
Verbatim tapes, optical and floppy disks. Your best defense against data loss.

Look on the bright side.
We know our data's
going to survive.
Verbatim
OPTICAL DISK
Verbatim tapes, optical and floppy disks. Your best defense against data loss.

We probably won't live to tell about it. But hey, our data will.
Verbatim
OPTICAL DISK
Verbatim tapes, optical and floppy disks. Your best defense against data loss.

REMEMBER
THE LAST TIME
THE OSHA
INSPECTOR
DROPPED BY?
HOW TO HAVE
A SUCCESSFUL OSHA
INSPECTION
A ONE DAY SEMINAR
SEPTEMBER 3, 1998
ASSOCIATION
OF
GENERAL
CONTRACTORS

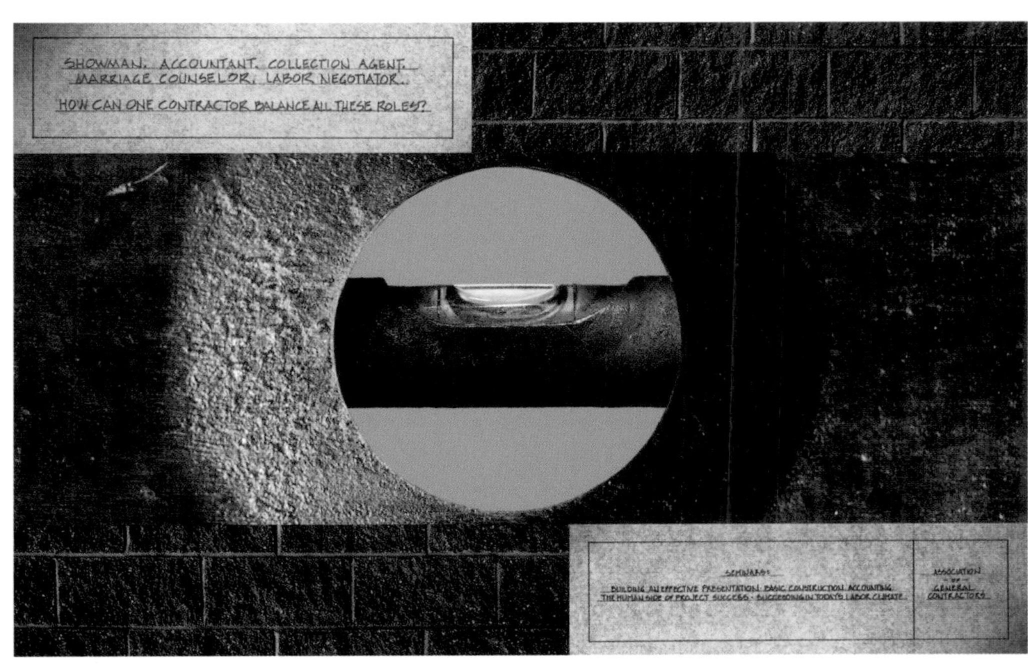
SHOWMAN. ACCOUNTANT. COLLECTION AGENT.
MARRIAGE COUNSELOR. LABOR NEGOTIATOR.
HOW CAN ONE CONTRACTOR BALANCE ALL THESE ROLES?
SEMINARS:
BUILDING AN EFFECTIVE PRESENTATION · BASIC CONSTRUCTION ACCOUNTING
THE HUMAN SIDE OF PROJECT SUCCESS · SUCCEEDING IN TODAY'S LABOR CLIMATE
ASSOCIATION
OF
GENERAL
CONTRACTORS

MAYBE NOW
WOULD BE A GOOD
TIME TO JOIN US
FOR OUR
LABOR RELATIONS
SEMINAR
SUCCEEDING IN TODAY'S
LABOR CLIMATE
AND OTHER RELATED
SEMINARS
ASSOCIATION
OF
GENERAL
CONTRACTORS

Odd as
it may seem
coming from
a museum
dedicated to
preservation
we're glad
it's extinct.
ACRO

Client: North Carolina Museum of Natural Sciences **Creative Director:** Jim Mountjoy **Art Director:** Doug Pedersen **Copywriter:** Curtis Smith **Account Executive:** Darren Brady-Harris **Photographer:** Pat Staub

HAND-ROLLED.
PUNGENT AROMA.
MILDLY MOOD-ALTERING.
AND YOU WON'T EVEN
CRAVE SNACK
FOODS AFTERWARDS.

THE CIGAR BAR AT ARTHUR'S

AFTER GOOD SEX.

AFTER GREAT SEX.

THE CIGAR BAR AT ARTHUR'S

NOBODY KNOWS COMICS LIKE WE DO
HEROES
Comics & Games

EMPLOYEE LOUNGE
NOBODY KNOWS COMICS LIKE WE DO
HEROES
aren't hard
TO FIND
Comics & Games
(704)-375-7462
heroesonline.com

POPULATION:
north
carolina
for a free travel guide,
call 1-800-VISIT NC

Client: (top) Heroes Aren't Hard to Find (bottom) North Carolina Travel & Tourism **Creative Director:** Jim Mountjoy **Art Director:** Doug Pedersen **Copywriter:** Curtis Smith **Account Executive:** (top) Jim Mountjoy (bottom) John Ketchum **Photographer:** (top) Pat Staub (bottom) Olaf Veltman

Loeffler Ketchum Mountj

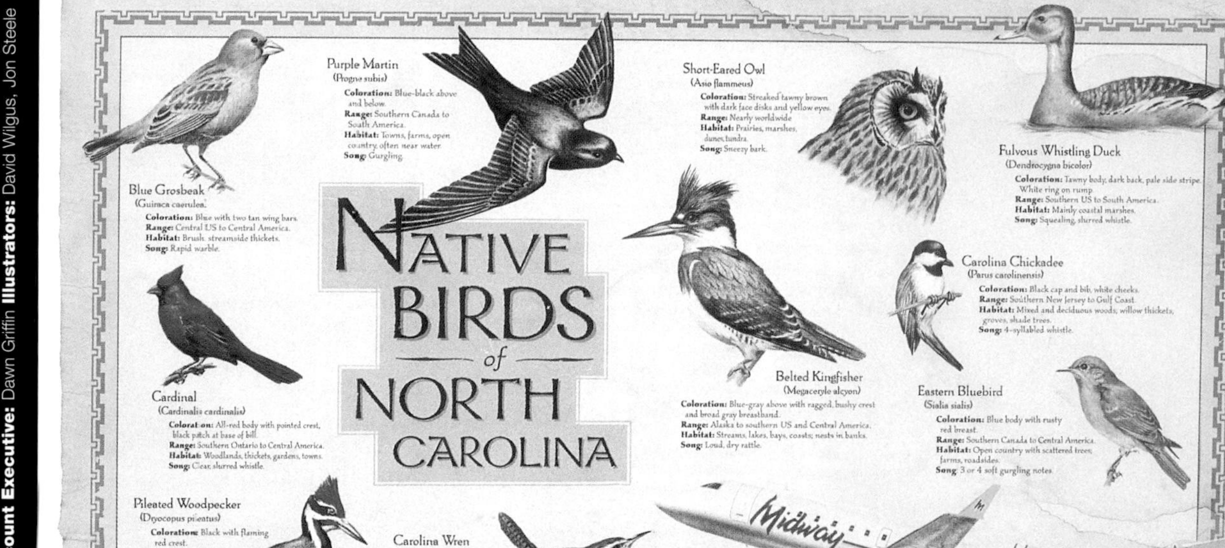

NATIVE BIRDS of NORTH CAROLINA
Blue Grosbeak
(Guiraca caerulea)
Coloration: Blue with two tan wing bars.
Range: Central US to Central America.
Habitat: Brush. streamside thickets.
Song: Rapid warble.
Purple Martin
(Progne subis)
Coloration: Blue-black above and below.
Range: Southern Canada to South America.
Habitat: Towns, farms, open country, often near water.
Song: Gurgling.
Short-Eared Owl
(Asio flammeus)
Coloration: Streaked tawny brown with dark face disks and yellow eyes.
Range: Nearly worldwide
Habitat: Prairies, marshes, dunes, tundra.
Song: Sneezy bark.
Fulvous Whistling Duck
(Dendrocygna bicolor)
Coloration: Tawny body, dark back, pale side stripe. White ring on rump.
Range: Southern US to South America.
Habitat: Mainly coastal marshes.
Song: Squealing, slurred whistle.
Cardinal
(Cardinalis cardinalis)
Coloration: All-red body with pointed crest, black patch at base of bill.
Range: Southern Ontario to Central America.
Habitat: Woodlands, thickets, gardens, towns.
Song: Clear, slurred whistle.
Carolina Chickadee
(Parus carolinensis)
Coloration: Black cap and bib, white cheeks.
Range: Southern New Jersey to Gulf Coast.
Habitat: Mixed and deciduous woods; willow thickets, groves, shade trees.
Song: 4-syllabled whistle.
Belted Kingfisher
(Megaceryle alcyon)
Coloration: Blue-gray above with ragged, bushy crest and broad gray breastband.
Range: Alaska to southern US and Central America.
Habitat: Streams, lakes, bays, coasts; nests in banks.
Song: Loud, dry rattle.
Eastern Bluebird
(Sialia sialis)
Coloration: Blue body with rusty red breast.
Range: Southern Canada to Central America.
Habitat: Open country with scattered trees; farms, roadsides.
Song 3 or 4 soft gurgling notes.
Pileated Woodpecker
(Dryocopus pileatus)
Coloration: Black with flaming red crest.
Range: Canada to southern US.
Habitat: Conifer, hardwood and mixed forests.
Song: Loud, ringing call
Carolina Wren
(Thryothorus ludovicianus)
Coloration: Warm reddish brown above, buff below. White eyebrow stripe.
Range: Eastern US and Mexico.
Habitat: Tangles, brush, suburban gardens, towns.
Song: 3-syllabled chant.
Midway
Midway Airlines CRJ
(Aerius carolinensis)
Coloration: White body, yellow tail with blue markings.
Range: East of Rockies to Eastern seaboard.
Habitat: Airports; nests in Raleigh/Durham.
Song: Low roar.
With more than 190 flights a day departing to destinations ranging from Boston, MA to Ft. Lauderdale, FL and all points in between, there's no better way to take flight from Raleigh/Durham. 1-800-44-MIDWAY
Midway AIRLINES
www.midwayair.com

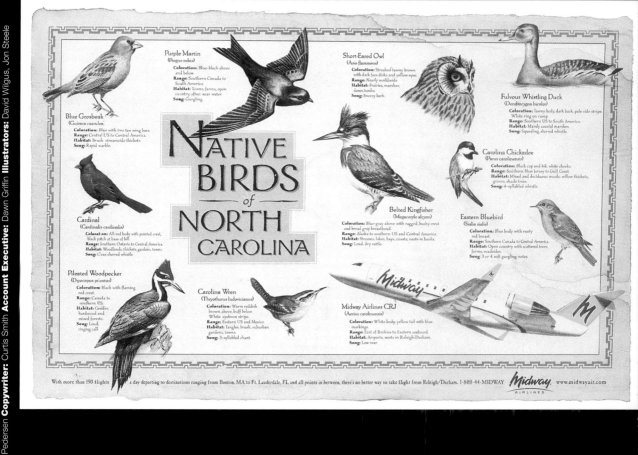

Director: Doug Pedersen **Copywriter:** Curtis Smith **Account Executive:** Dawn Griffin **Illustrators:** David Wilgus, Jon Steele

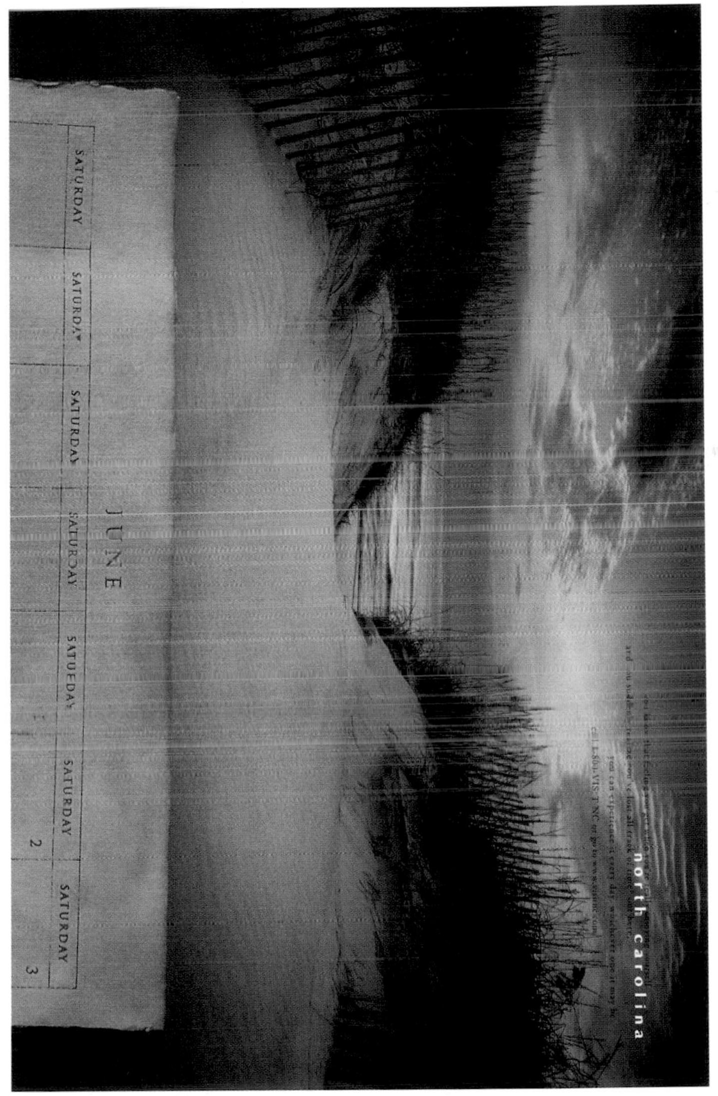

Client: North Carolina Travel & Tourism **Creative Director:** Jim Mountjoy **Art Director:** Doug Pedersen **Copywriter:** Curtis Smith **Account Executive:** John Ketchum **Photographer:** Olaf Veltman

Page 110 *The One Club* Ask creative people to rank the importance as well as the difficulty of winning awards and the result is pretty consistent. We decided to make that our concept. Bull's-eye.
Page 111 *Outward Bound* Outward Bound was perceived as stodgy and old. So we immersed ourselves in the world of our 14-21 year old audience. The result: "Tell me the truth," "Challenge me," "Make me go beyond myself." The client made changes to their courses. We made changes to the messages. It's working.
Page 112 *VELUX-America Inc.* VELUX sells the world's finest skylights and roof windows. That's the product. But the real benefit is that they bring you the sky.
Page 113 *Mannington Floors* Every floor ad does the same thing. Show room. Show floor. Nobody stands out. So when Mannington introduced a new vinyl floor with the look and feel of real mosaic tile, something as unique as the floor itself needed to be done. It was a hit. So was the floor.
Page 114-115 *Verbatim* Data storage disks are all alike. But that doesn't mean their advertising has to be. Against the scientific technobabble of their competitors, we gave Verbatim a "fun but trusting" personality in the world of zeros and ones. The message, "no matter what happens, your data's safe," was demonstrated through extreme and unusual circumstances.
Page 116 *Carolinas AGC Inc.* Contractors and builders consistently put on seminars and training programs to raise the level of quality in all facets of their work. CAGC is the association responsible for this. We used their language and look to promote the association's programs.
Page 117 *North Carolina Museum of Natural Sciences* T-Rex was bad. Acro was badder. Acro was several tons of attitude that came to a razor point of teeth and claws. All of our work for the museum focused on the drama that was inherent in that ferociousness.
Page 118 *Arthur's* Smoking is bad for you. It's politically incorrect. It's unsightly. It disturbs people. Makes them uncomfortable. Perfect. A product that knows what it is and isn't, and knows that failure is predicated on trying to please everybody.
Page 119 (top) *Heroes Aren't Hard to Find* The next best thing to all the fantastic characters on comic book store shelves are all the fantastic characters who hang around comic book stores. (bottom) *North Carolina Travel & Tourism* Everything we do for North Carolina rests on one single position: Natural scenic beauty in a restful, relaxing atmosphere. All of North Carolina's work is driven by that position, and has been for over 10 years.
Page 120 *Midway Airlines* Midway wants to be North Carolina's airline. Its efforts and marketing reflect that. So when we were asked to do an in-state magazine ad, this was a natural.
Page 121 *North Carolina Travel & Tourism* Everything we do for North Carolina rests on one single position: Natural scenic beauty in a restful, relaxing atmosphere. All of North Carolina's work is driven by that position, and has been for over 10 years.

2101 Rexford Foad, Suite 200 East Charlotte, North Carolina 28211 tel. 704-364-8969 fax. 704-364-8470

Ogilvy&Mather

PESCADO!

Ogilvy&Mather

The defining quality of Ogilvy & Mather is its devotion to brands. The company's stated mission, "To be Most Valued by Those Who Most Value Brands," articulates a point of view that goes back to the principles of David Ogilvy, the agency's legendary founder. "Every advertisement must contribute to the long term health of the brand." Ogilvy said those words in 1955, and they form the philosophical bedrock that has supported the company's steady growth. Now, just over 50 years old, it has become one of the largest multi-disciplined agency networks in the world, with 483 offices in 106 countries.■Most importantly, this commitment to the brand has given the agency a defining point of view on the nature of its service to clients, and how it goes about delivering it. Ogilvy believes that every thing it does to build its client's brand must be based on a deep and abiding understanding of how these brands live in the hearts and minds of consumers. Stated simply, the agency's job is to be the steward of the brand relationship with the consumer. This point of view has been of great advantage as the business of marketing has changed dramatically. Today's globalization of brands, the ensuing ferocious competition, the inability for most brands to sustain product advantage, the explosion of media channels, and the one-to-one revolutionary nature of the internet have created an environment that requires a more multi-discipline approach to the consumer. Today, as brand stewards, agencies must be willing and able to connect to the consumer by using more channels than ever before, and to ensure that those different moments of contact add up to an enriched experience. Ogilvy calls this strategy, 360° Brand Stewardship. It is a philosophy and a practice that is supported by a host of proprietary tools and techniques employed in every Ogilvy office around the world.■Philosophy and practice are just two legs of the stool; the key to making 360° Branding effective is creativity. Shelly Lazarus, Chairman and CEO of Ogilvy, has said, "If Brand Stewardship doesn't result in great creative, then it has failed its mission." And Rick Boyko, Chief Creative Officer of Ogilvy North America believes that in order to execute a 360° campaign, the agency needs to think in a 360° manner. Where there is great reverence for the brand and a devotion to understanding how the brand lives in people's lives, Ogilvy believes there will be inspired creative solutions. Where there is a belief that the consumer absorbs information about the brand in a variety of ways, opportunities will be found to create campaigns that leverage the power of the vast new array of media. Where the consumer increasingly is in control of the dialogue, only great, brand-perfect creativity will be meaningful. The central role creativity plays throughout the Ogilvy network is evidenced by the fact that more of Ogilvy's offices contribute to its creative reputation than any other agency network. It's not a few special talents; it's a process that is in place that has helped Ogilvy develop one of the deepest creative benches in the county. And it shows in the work.

top: Jeroen Bours (left) and David Apicella (right); bottom: Chris Wall (left) and Rick Boyko (right)

Client: Perrier **Creative Directors:** Rick Boyko, Glen Jacobs **Art Director:** Dave Laden **Copywriter:** Chris Mitton **Account Executives:** Shona Seifert, Peter Brodnitz **Photographer:** Vincent Dixon **Strategy:** Laurie Pollock

12
Perrier
©1999 Great Waters of France

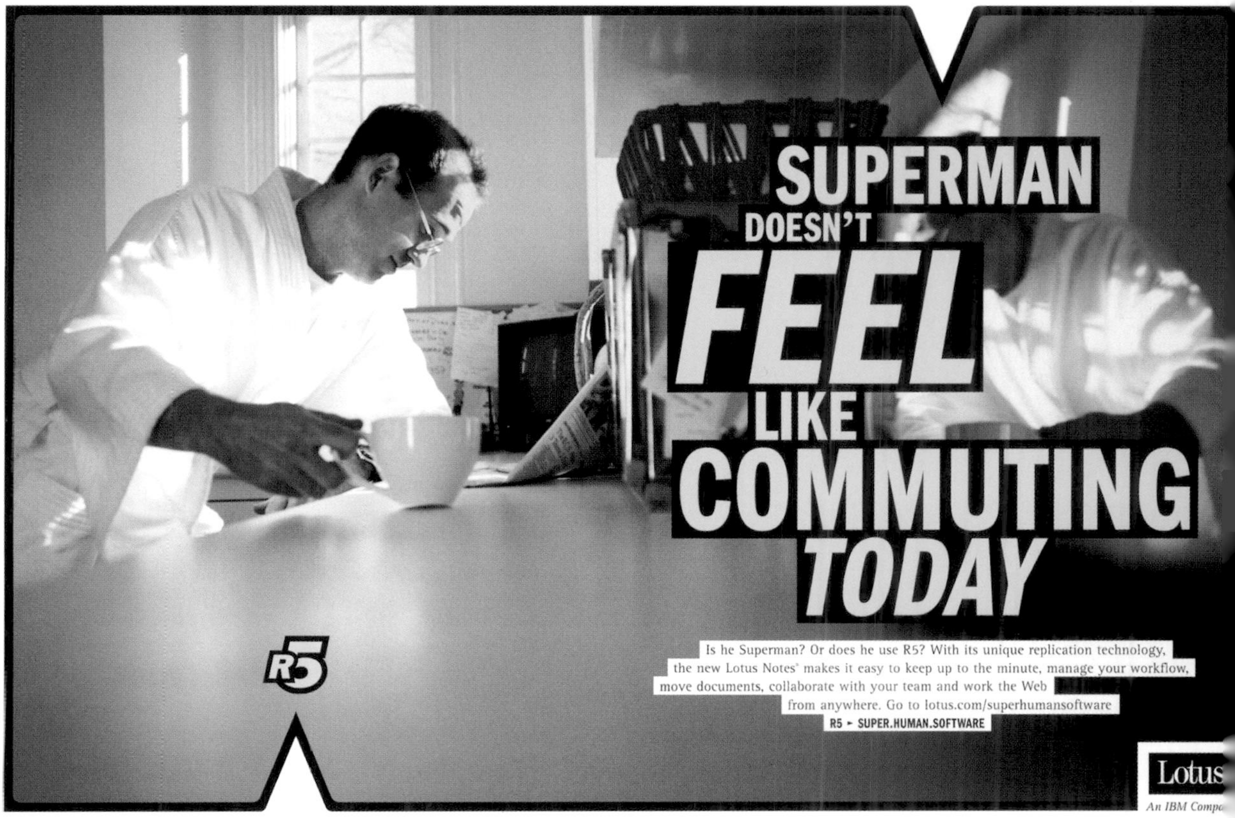

SUPERMAN
DOESN'T
FEEL
LIKE
COMMUTING
TODAY
R5
Is he Superman? Or does he use R5? With its unique replication technology,
the new Lotus Notes® makes it easy to keep up to the minute, manage your workflow,
move documents, collaborate with your team and work the Web
from anywhere. Go to lotus.com/superhumansoftware
R5 ► SUPER.HUMAN.SOFTWARE
Lotus
An IBM Compa

Lotus
An IBM Company
HAVING
SAVED
THE DAY
IN THREE TIME ZONES
SUPERMAN
TAKES A MOMENT TO
PONDER
THE NEXT MOVE
Is she Superman? Or does she use Lotus Notes® and Domino™ R5? Notes and Domino make it
easy for team members, inside and outside your organization, all around the world,
to share up-to-the-minute information. So you can get products to market faster,
improve customer satisfaction and save money. Go to lotus.com/superhumansoftware
SUPER.HUMAN.SOFTWARE

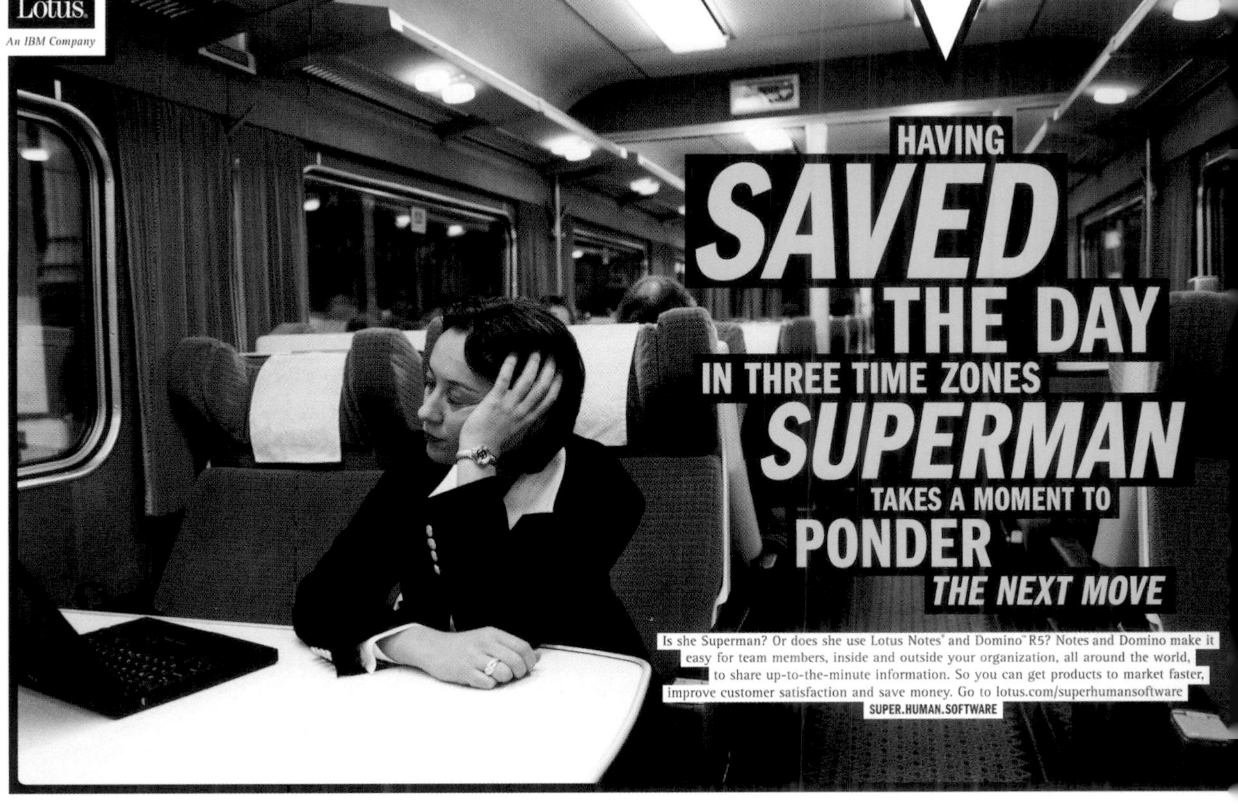

Client: Lotus **Creative Directors:** Chris Wall, Tony Arefin **Art Director:** Chris Curry **Copywriter:** Brendan Gibbons **Account Executives:** Danielle Keary, Mary Tetlow **Photographer:** Jake Chessum

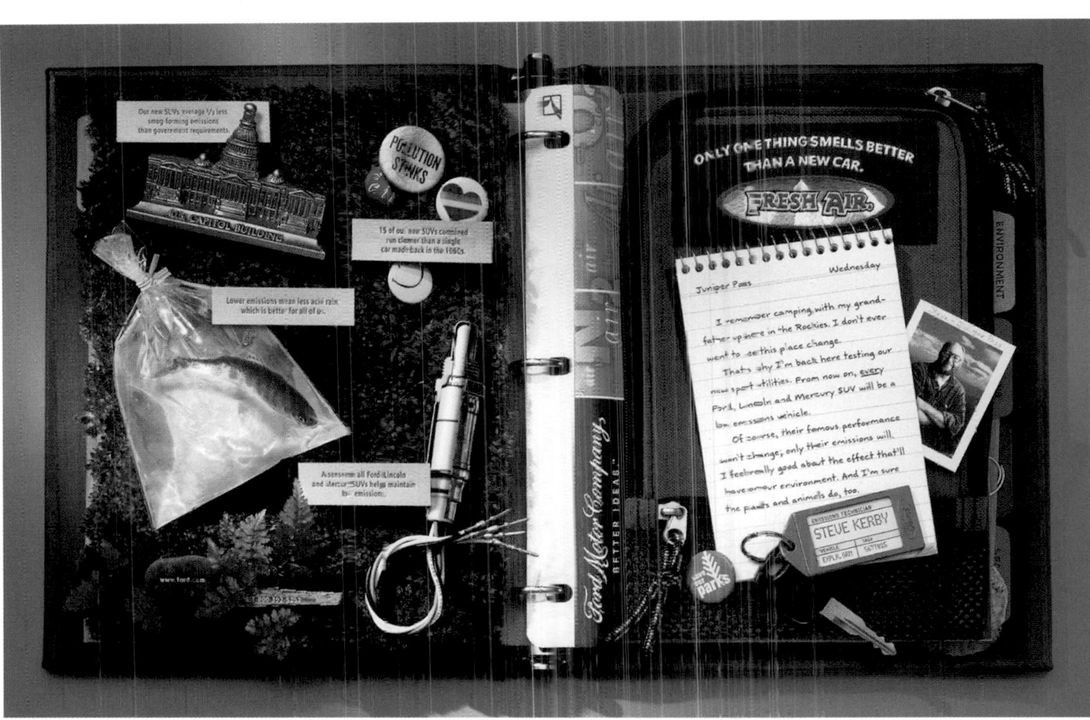

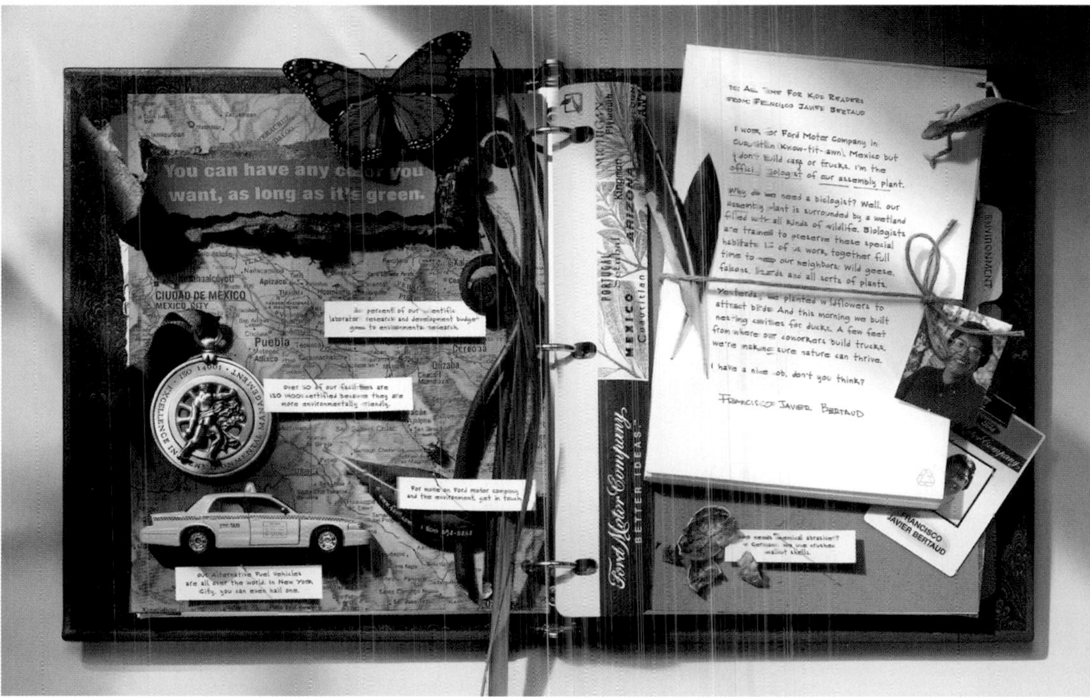

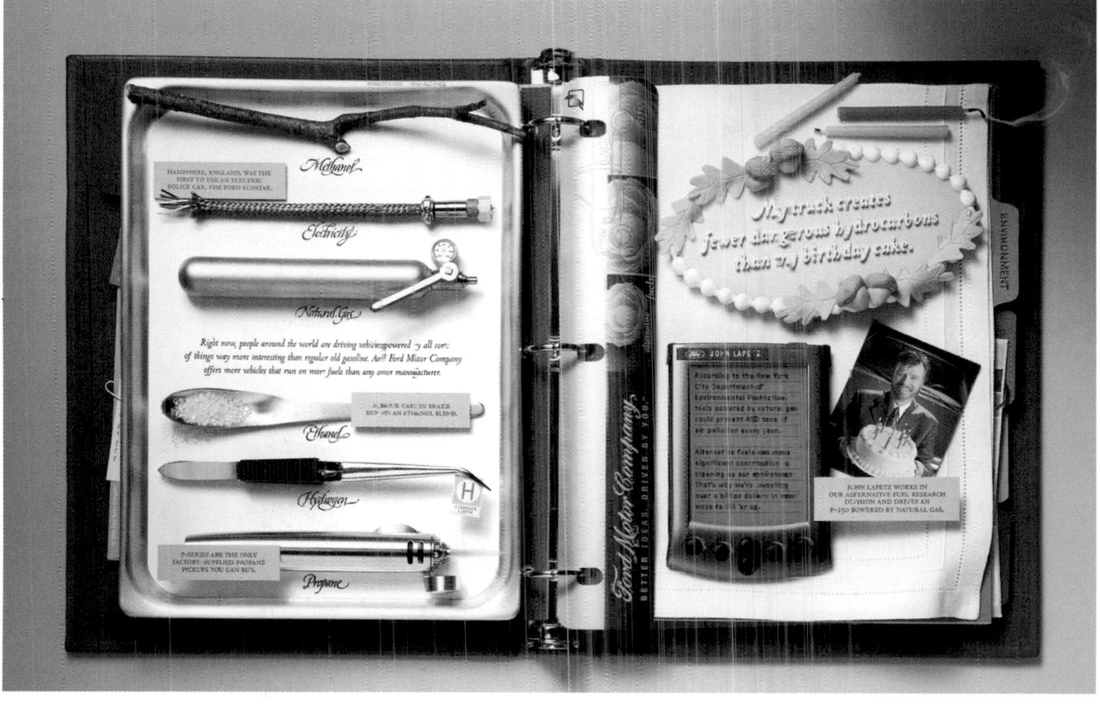

Client: Ford Motor Company **Creative Director:** Ross Sutherland **Art Directors:** Grant Parrish, Marwan Khuri **Designers:** Grant Parrish, Marwan Khuri, Marino Gallo **Copywriters:** Danny Gregory, Jim Nolan, Jill Applebaum **Print Producer:** John Gregorio **Typographer:** Robert Wakeman **Account Executives:** Richard Bohner-Davies, Tim Jones **Photographer:** Lisa Charles Watson

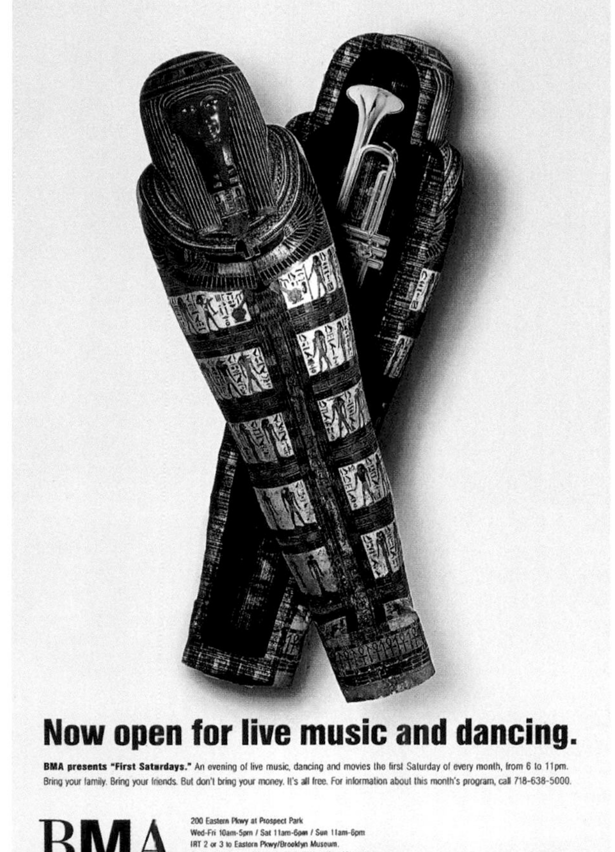

Now open for live music and dancing.
BMA presents "First Saturdays." An evening of live music, dancing and movies the first Saturday of every month, from 6 to 11pm. Bring your family. Bring your friends. But don't bring your money. It's all free. For information about this month's program, call 718-638-5000.
BMA
200 Eastern Pkwy at Prospect Park
Wed-Fri 10am-5pm / Sat 11am-6pm / Sun 11am-6pm
IRT 2 or 3 to Eastern Pkwy/Brooklyn Museum.
On site parking. 718.638.5000. http://www.brooklynart.org
Brooklyn Museum of Art

Not your typical evening at the museum.
BMA presents "First Saturdays." An evening of live music, dancing and movies the first Saturday of every month, from 6 to 11pm. Bring your family. Bring your friends. But don't bring your money. It's all free. For information about this month's program, call 718-638-5000.
BMA
200 Eastern Pkwy at Prospect Park
Wed-Fri 10am-5pm / Sat 11am-6pm / Sun 11am-6pm
IRT 2 or 3 to Eastern Pkwy/Brooklyn Museum.
On site parking. 718.638.5000. http://www.brooklynart.org
Brooklyn Museum of Art

Client: Brooklyn Museum of Art **Creative Director:** Bruce Lee **Art Director:** Alfredo Rossi **Copywriter:** Mark Drossman **Illustrator:** Brooklyn Museum of Art, Magic Graphics

WE COVER THE MEDIA.

WE ALSO *UNCOVER* THE MEDIA.

BRILLS CONTENT

SKEPTICISM IS A VIRTUE

AN ADULT MAGAZINE *WITHOUT* ALL THAT

ANNOYING NAKED STUFF.

BRILLS CONTENT

SKEPTICISM IS A VIRTUE

THIN-SKINNED,

SELF-RIGHTEOUS MEDIA MOGULS THINK WE'RE TRASH.

AND THE *THICK-SKINNED* ONES

AREN'T TOO THRILLED WITH US, EITHER.

BRILLS CONTENT

SKEPTICISM IS A VIRTUE

WRITING ARTICLES

ON *LIPOSUCTION* AND *TANTRIC SEX*

DOESN'T INTEREST US.

BUT A STORY ON UNATTRIBUTED QUOTES IN THE MEDIA?

COME TO PAPA.

BRILLS CONTENT

SKEPTICISM IS A VIRTUE

Client: Brill's Content **Associate Creative Directors:** Josh Tavlin, John McNeil **Art Directors:** (top, left and right) Mark Graham (bottom, left and right) John McNeil **Copywriters:** (top, left and right) Kristen Steele (bottom, left and right) Josh Tavlin

Client: Hershey Chocolate/Jolly Rancher **Creative Directors:** David Apicella, Jeroen Bours **Art Directors:** Alex Fallon, Robyn Sands **Designer:** Paul Hoyne **Copywriters:** Robyn Sands, Alex Fallon **Account Executives:** Charlie Armstrong, Amy Robertson **Photographer:** James Wojzik

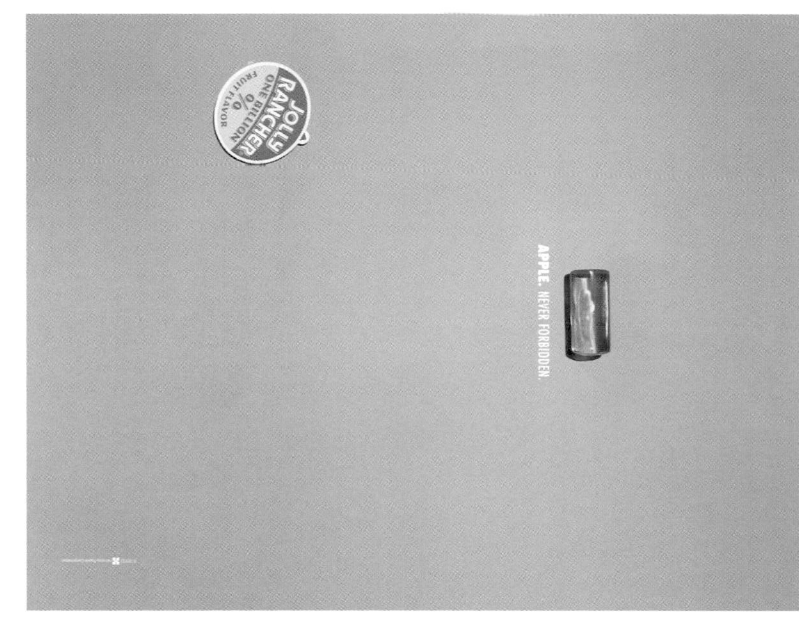

Client: Kraft Foods **Creative Directors:** Rick Boyko, Kevin Kelly, Terril Smith **Art Director:** Garrett Jewett **Designer:** Garrett Jewett **Copywriter:** Lisa Mayer **Account Executives:** Bob Hay, Darren Kapelus, Arabella Decker **Photographers:** Photonica and FPG (wheat field and sky), Beth Galton (cereal)

Client: IBM **Creative Director:** Chris Wall **Associate Creative Directors:** Josh Tavlin, John McNeil **Art Director:** John McNeil, Mark Graham, Arturo Gigante **Copywriter:** Victoria Ludwin **Photographer:** Robert Lewis

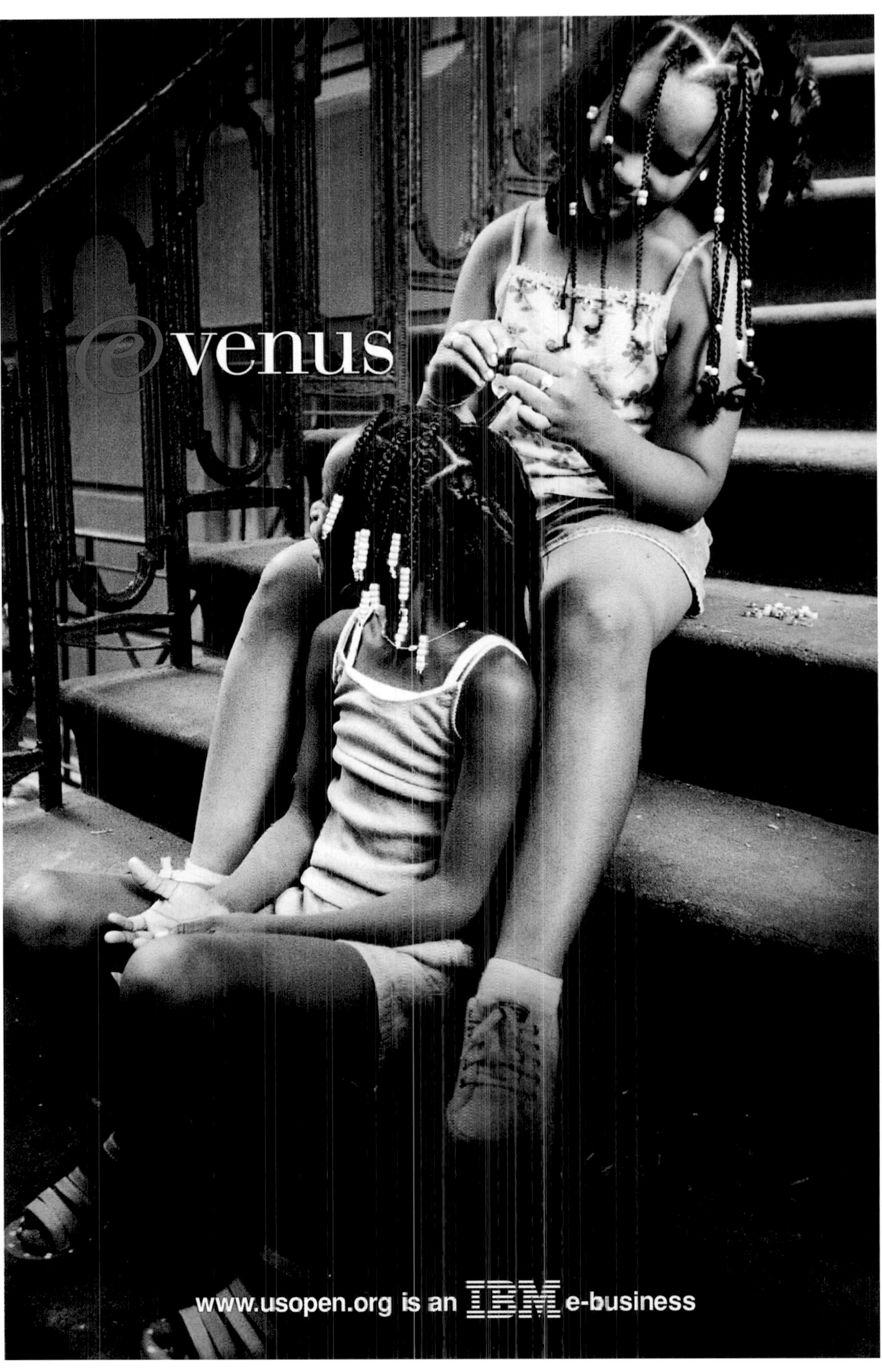

@venus
www.usopen.org is an IBM e-business

Creative Director: Chris Wall **Associate Creative Directors:** Josh Tavlin, John McNeil **Art Directors:** John McNeil, Jeff Compton **Copywriter:** Victoria Ludwin **Account Executives:** Rebecca Wright, Laura Pryskulnik **Photographer:** Nitin Vadukul

Client: IBM

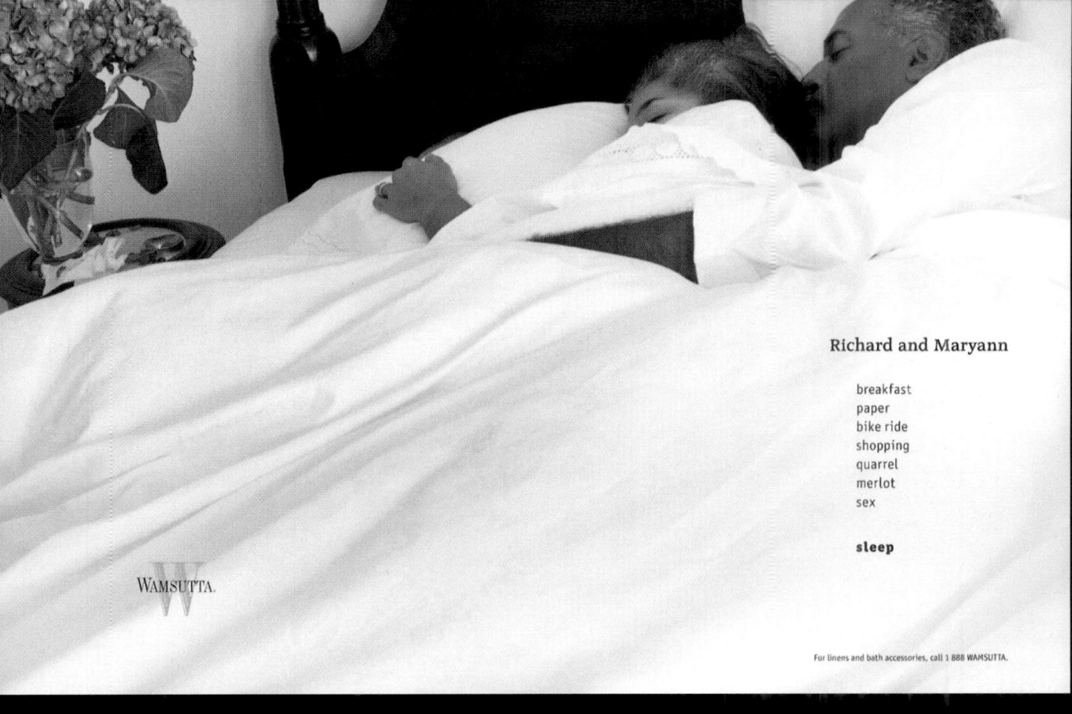
Richard and Maryann
breakfast
paper
bike ride
shopping
quarrel
merlot
sex
sleep
WAMSUTTA
For linens and bath accessories, call 1 888 WAMSUTTA.

Diane
give away kittens
write poem
tear up poem
swim
cheesecake
pedicure
sleep
WAMSUTTA
For linens and bath accessories, call 1 888 WAMSUTTA.

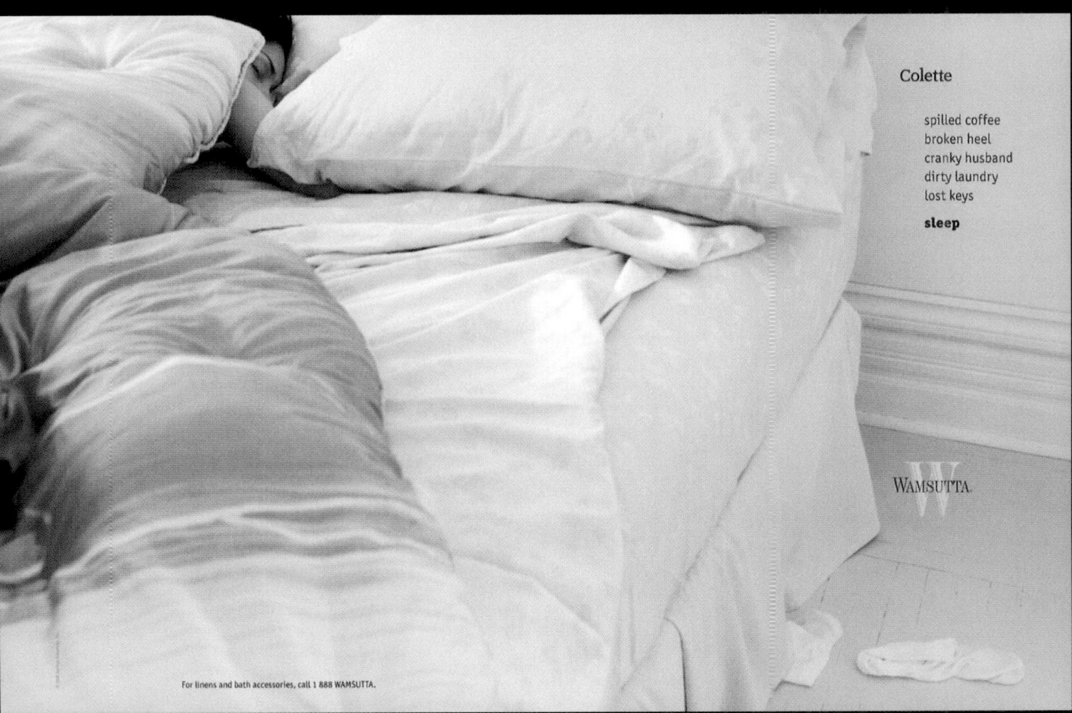
Colette
spilled coffee
broken heel
cranky husband
dirty laundry
lost keys
sleep
WAMSUTTA
For linens and bath accessories, call 1 888 WAMSUTTA.

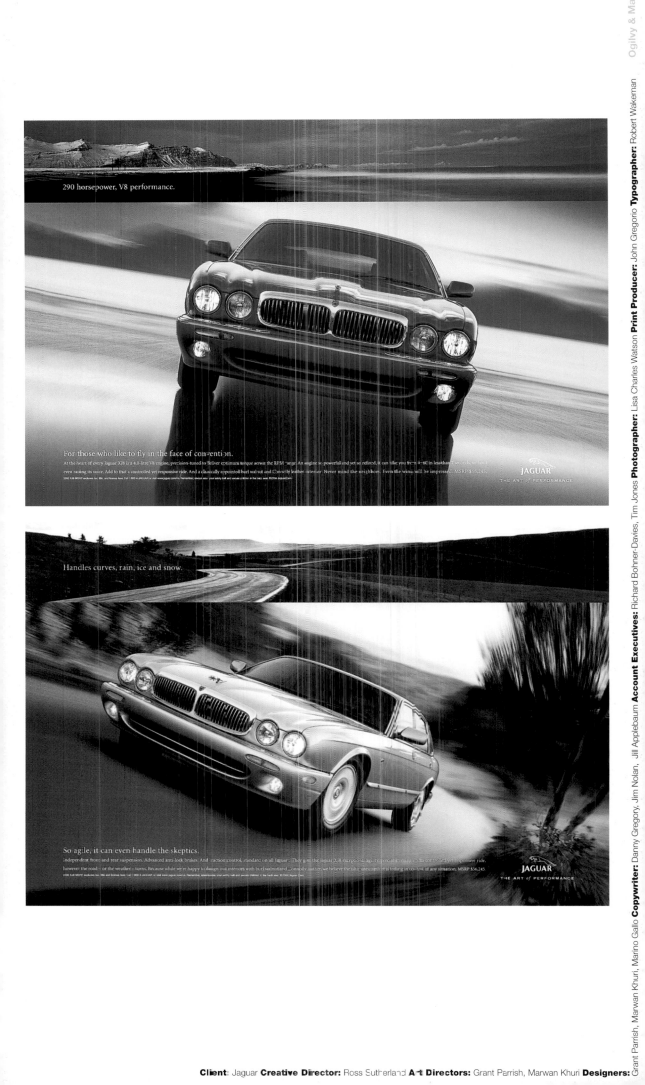

Client: Jaguar **Creative Director:** Ross Sutherland **Art Directors:** Grant Parrish, Marwan Khuri **Designers:** Grant Parrish, Marwan Khuri, Marino Gallo **Copywriter:** Danny Gregory, Jim Nolan, Jill Applebaum **Account Executives:** Richard Bohner-Davies, Tim Jones **Photographer:** Lisa Charles Watson **Print Producer:** John Gregorio **Typographer:** Robert Wakeman

Page 126-127 *Perrier* This campaign for Perrier was created by Ogilvy & Mather in Paris. In conjunction with their work, this execution was developed by the New York office for the American market. The campaign demonstrates the refreshment and irreverence of this famous brand by depicting various characters on t-shirts. They interact with the Perrier in front of them and express the wearer's thirst and desire for it. The work was designed to appeal to a younger audience, which is also reflected in the media used, which combined print with wild postings and postcards.

Page 128 *Lotus* The launch of Lotus Notes R5 was the chance for Lotus to reassert its traditional role as an innovator and leader in both business software and personal computing. Under the banner of Super.Human.Software, Lotus had its most successful year ever. A totally integrated campaign—part of Ogilvy's 360-degree approach to everything—with TV, interactive, direct mail and these outdoor boards made "I am superman" a rallying cry among Notes users.

Page 129 *Ford Motor Company* In this campaign, Ford Motor Company put forth its environmental accomplishments in an interesting and believable way. The notebook was designed to have the message come from an employee and to present lots of different ideas quickly and easily. The target group included consumers, environmental leaders, and the many employees of Ford Motor Company.

Page 130 *Brooklyn Museum of Art* This ad was created by Ogilvy One. Only a short time before New York City Mayor Rudy Giuliani brought plenty of unintended free publicity to the Brooklyn Museum in response to its controversial "Sensation" exhibit, the museum wanted to sharply increase its attendance levels. Because it's located outside of Manhattan, the institution was considered too far off the beaten path by most museum-goers. And the people who lived in its immediate vicinity simply weren't interested in what the museum had to offer. To attract new visitors and change the locals' perceptions, the BMA came up with a series of free after-hours events to be held the first Saturday of every month. To promote these events, the creatives at Ogilvy developed this campaign to communicate the fun, surprisingly casual, "let your hair down" nature of these evenings. The campaign, and thus "First Saturdays" itself, was a stunning success. In fact, so many people were showing up at the museum's doors each month that the ads had to be pulled.

Page 131 *Brill's Content* We needed to clarify the magazine's positioning—to create ads that reflected the magazine's smart, aggresive, "question authority" ethos. In this case, the authority is the media.

Page 132 *Hershey Chocolate/Jolly Rancher* To highlight the big bright intense flavor of Jolly Rancher candies, we used bold full color pages and quick, clever headlines. The colors correspond to the flavors, green for green apple, red for watermelon, etc. The huge sticker borrows from fruit labels, and also emphasizes the bold fruit flavor.

Page 133 *Kraft Foods* The goal here was to tap into a growing consumer appreciation of simple and straightforward solutions. It doesn't get any simpler than Shredded Wheat. Some consumers even refer to it as "raw" wheat in a box. The visual similarity between a wheat field and the Shredded Wheat biscuits reinforces the consumer perception that all the goodness of 100% wheat goes into every box.

Page 134-135 *IBM* The IBM e-business campaign has fundamentally changed the world's perception of IBM and how the company fits into the future. The campaign, launched in the fall of 1997, has made e-business part of the contemporary language. Its familiar blue letterbox TV spots and outdoor and print like these have given the company a new voice and fresh momentum to compete in an internet world.

Page 136 *Wamsutta* Quiet, intimate, young, fashionable, intense - these extremely personal ads gave a new, more contemporary twist to the venerable Wamsutta brand and helped them compete effectively against designer brands.

Page 137 *Jaguar* Launching the XJ Series from Jaguar with performance in mind. Previous XJ work had focused on the car's beauty and status appeal; in the new ads, we also wanted people to see it as a serious performance automobile.

309 West 49th Street New York, NY 10019 tel. 212-237-4000 fax. 237-5123

Saatchi&Saatchi

Saatchi & Saatchi New Zealand has been in existence since 1988. We have offices in Auckland and Wellington, and we are the largest and consistently most successful agency in the country. Although the agency is small by international standards, and located on the edge of the world, we aspire to be world class. ■ We see ourselves as an ideas company. Our ambition is for our ideas to transform the businesses, brands and reputations of our clients. We work differently than other agencies. Our thinking is based on the idea of defining the Challenge for the Idea. ■ What sort of partnerships are we seeking to build for the brand? We work with many of New Zealand's leading companies, including Telecom New Zealand, Lion Breweries, the New Zealand Dairy Foods and Westpac Trust. Internationally, we also work with Adidas—last year launching their sponsorship of the All Blacks in over 50 countries, and this year creating an online game for them. ■ Any agency's success is founded on its culture. Ours is best summed up by Five Golden Rules, which are the mantra we live by: 1. Never settle for second best. 2. Surround yourself with good people. 3. Work with clients who are equally passionate. 4. Show respect for consumers by rewarding them with great ideas. 5. Believe that nothing is impossible.

John McCabe (top left) and Gavin Bradley (top right)

Malsey, Len Cheeseman **Copywriters:** Nigel Richardson, Oliver Malsey **Account Supervisors:** Geoff Ross, Andrea Hammond **Typographers:** Len Cheeseman, Haycen Doughty **Digital Imaging:**

Client: Aukland Regional Council **Art Director and Copywriter:** Andrew Tinning **Account Supervisor:** James Ward

A crisp clean bite

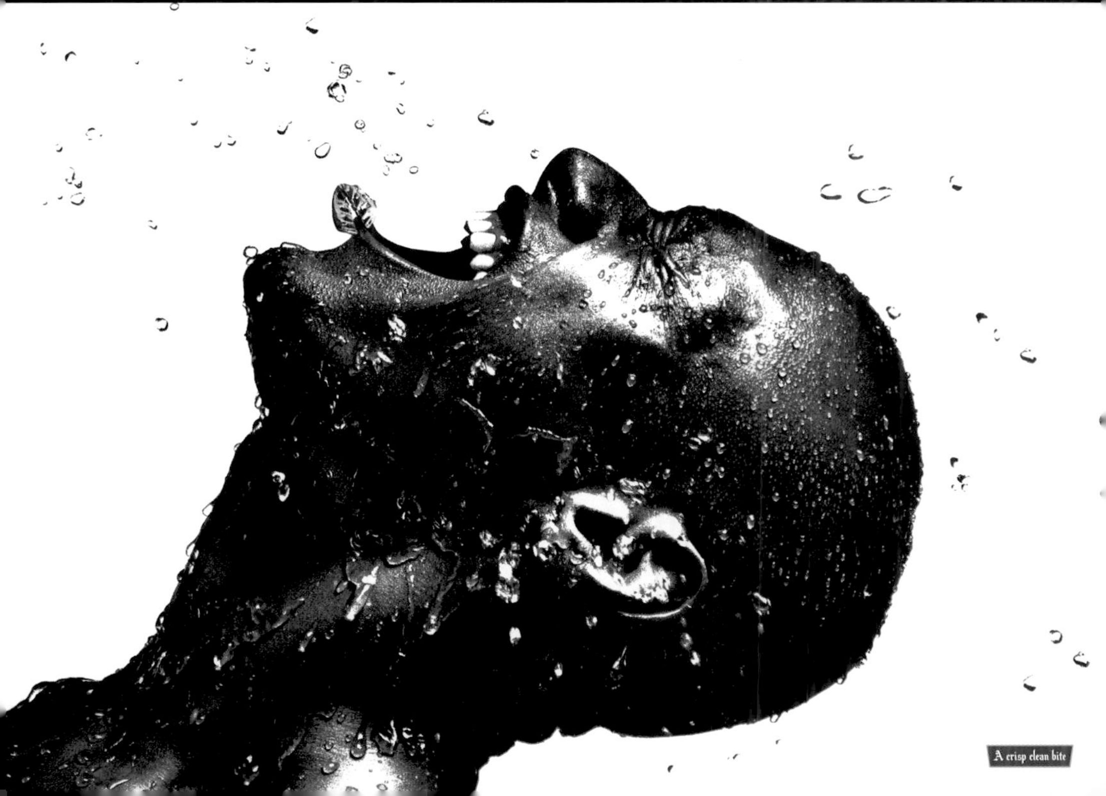

A crisp clean bite

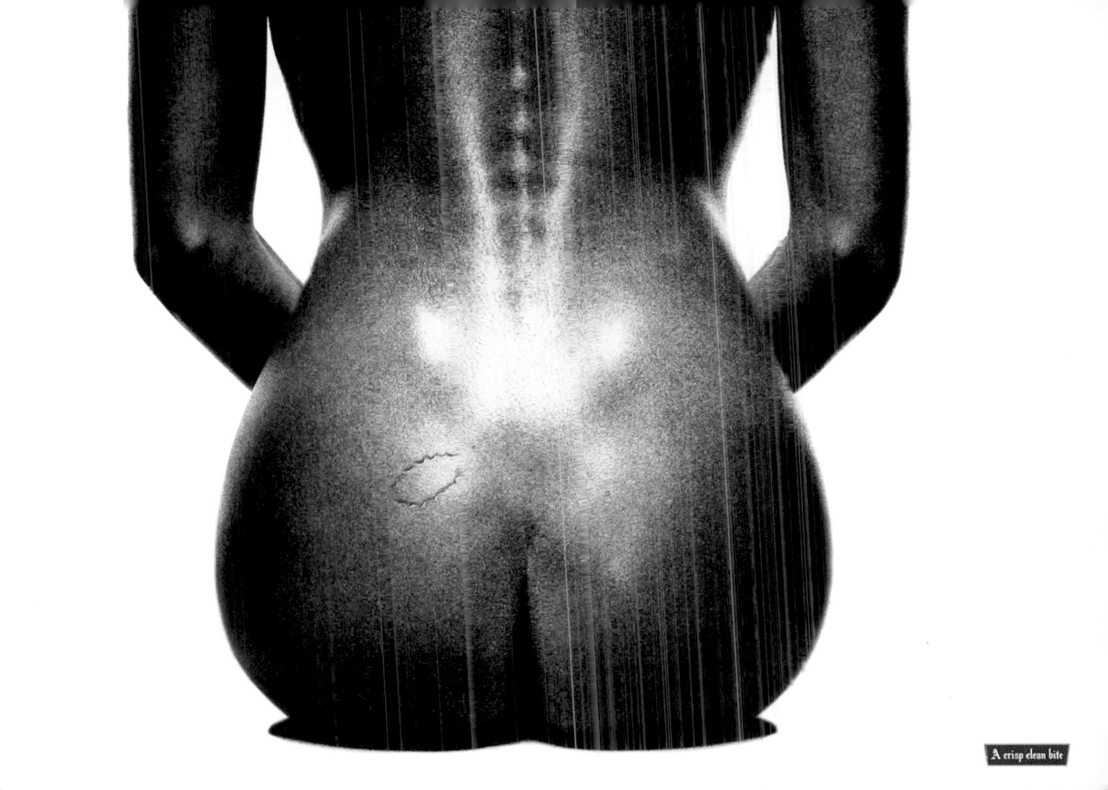

A crisp clean bite

A crisp clean bite

ONLY ONE THING
STOPS
THE RED CROSS
NEW ZEALAND RED CROSS
THE STAFF AND VOLUNTEERS OF THE RED CROSS ARE NOT EASILY FRIGHTENED. WHERE HELP IS
NEEDED, WE HAVE A REPUTATION FOR BEING THE FIRST TO ENTER A DISASTER AREA AND THE LAST
TO LEAVE. AS A RESULT WE'RE OFTEN THE ONE INTERNATIONAL RELIEF AGENCY REMAINING IN PARTS
OF THE WORLD THAT HAVE LONG LEFT THE HEADLINES. IN FACT
THE LIVES OF OUR WORKERS ARE DIRECTLY THREATENED.
DIFFICULT OR DANGEROUS BUT IF THOSE WHO DEPEND ON US ARE TO

HOW TO SAY
"DON'T SHOOT
ME" IN 350
LANGUAGES
THE IDEA FOR THE RED CROSS EMBLEM WAS BORN ON A BATTLEFIELD IN SOLFERINO
IN 1859. TODAY IT STILL SEPARATES MEDICS FROM SOLDIERS, LIFE FROM DEATH. IT IS
PROTECTED BY GENEVA CONVENTION AND TO MISUSE IT IS A CRIME UNDER LAW. IT DOESN'T
BELONG ON A FIRST AID KIT. IT CAN'T BE USED BY VETS OR MEDICAL CENTRES. IT IS
A SYMBOL OF PROTECTION, NEUTRALITY AND HUMANITY. THE NEW ZEALAND RED
CROSS HAS A DUTY TO PROTECT IT, BECAUSE WITHOUT IT WE CAN'T PROTECT YOU.

Client: New Zealand Red Cross **Creative Director:** Kim Thorp **Art Directors:** Len Cheeseman, Evan Purdie **Copywriters:** Ken Double, Steve Cooper **Account Supervisors:** Linda Jones, Bridgette Yates **Photographer:** Tony Squares **Illustrator:** Evan Purdie **Typographers:** Len Cheeseman, Carl Kennard

(This page, left) **Client:** New Zealand Children & Young Persons Service **Creative Director:** Kim Thorp **Art Director:** John Fisher **Copywriter:** John Plimme **Account Supervisors:** Wendy Schrijvers, Helen Tweedie **Digital Imaging:** Andy Salisbury **Typographer:** Len Cheeseman (This page, right) **Client:** Strok Foundation **Creative Director:** Gavin Bradley **Art Directors:** Len Cheeseman, John Fisher **Copywriter:** John Plimmer **Account Supervisor:** David Hendr **Illustrator:** Evan Purdie **Typographer:** Hayden Doughty **Digital Imaging:** Andy Salisbury

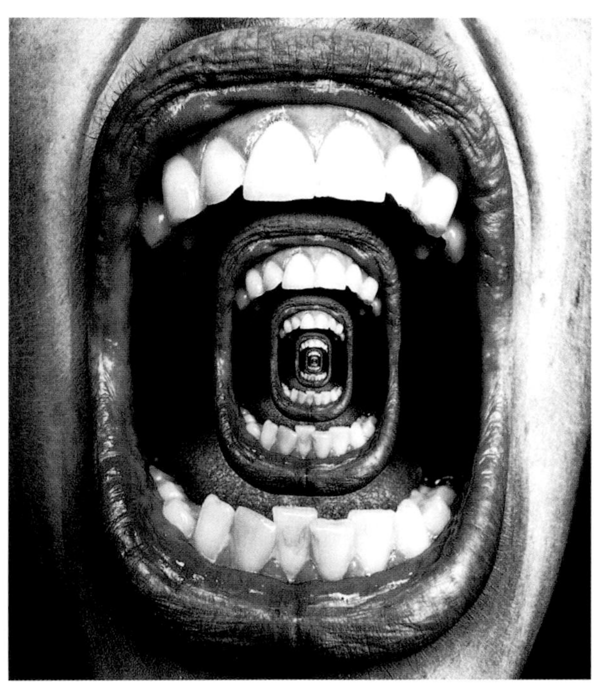

THE ABUSE YOU YELL
AT YOUR KIDS STAYS IN THE
FAMILY FOR GENERATIONS
You're useless. You're dumb. I wish you'd never been born. Shout verbal abuse like this at your kids and you don't just hurt them, you teach them to be abusive parents too. Break the cycle. Call 0800 222 999 for a free parenting booklet that will help.

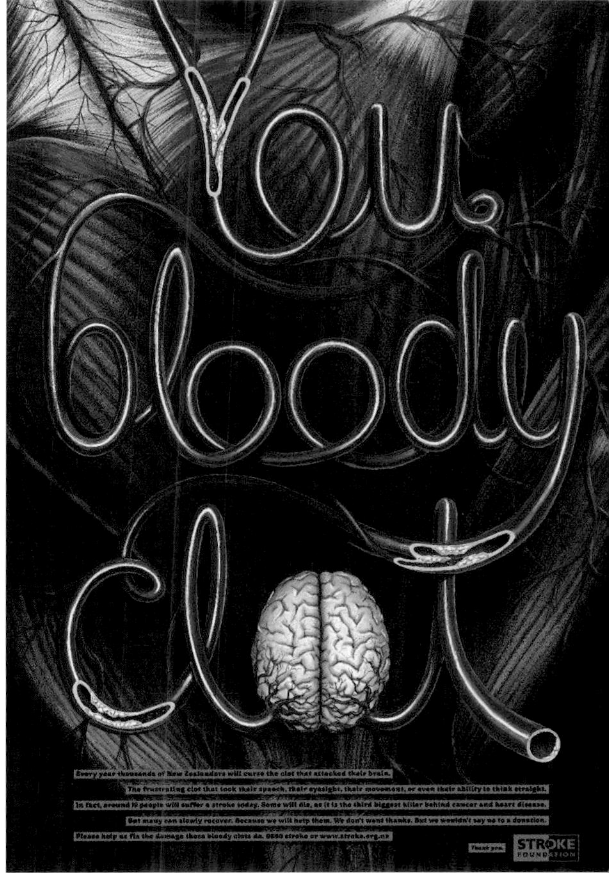

You bloody clot
Every year thousands of New Zealanders will curse the clot that attacked their brain.
The frustrating clot that took their speech, their eyesight, their movement, or even their ability to think straight.
But many can slowly recover. Because we will help them. We don't want thanks. But we wouldn't say no to a donation.
Thank you.
STROKE FOUNDATION

(Opposite, left) **Client:** AIDS Foundation of New Zealand **Creative Director:** Kim Thorp **Art Director:** Chris Bleakey **Copywriter:** Maggie Mouat **Acc Supervisors:** Maggie Mouat, Chris Bleakey **Typographer:** Eric de Vries (Opposite, right) **Client:** State of the World Forum **Creative Director:** Gavin Bradle **Director:** Steve Cooper **Copywriters:** Ken Double, Maggie Mouat **Account Supervisors:** Ian Christie, Angela Barnett **Typographers:** Len Cheeseman, H Doughty **Digital Imaging:** Andy Salisbury

Dear Eric,

There is a virus spreading through our community which is claiming a life every week. It is spread through contaminated blood or sexual contact. I'm sure you know what I'm talking about. HIV and ultimately AIDS.

The only way we can stop it spreading is to spread the word faster than the virus.

And the word is condoms. Practise safe sex and use them. It's that simple.

Now take this letter and copy it 6 times. Send them to people who you consider make the world a better place. Don't be embarrased, we could all do with a reminder.

If you send the letter on to six people this week, and each of these people do the same, by the end of the month 7,776 people will be better informed. If you choose to do nothing, by the end of the year several million people will have missed our message.

We owe it to everyone to spread the word and beat the virus.

SIGNED: Someone who cares

PS. If you could afford to send a donation to the Aids Foundation they would very much appreciate it. Their address is:

NZ AIDS Foundation.
PO Box 7287,
Wellington,
New Zealand.

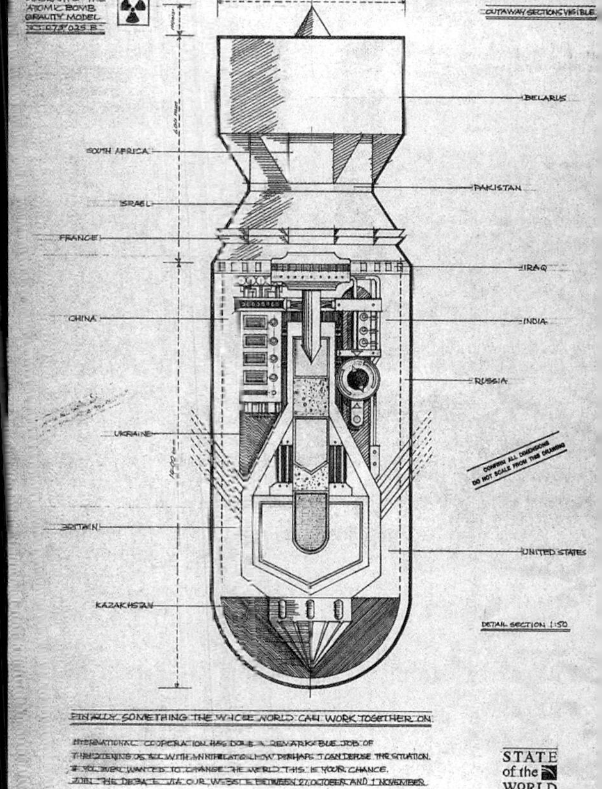

Client: Land Transport Safety Authority **Creative Director:** Gavin Bradley **Art Director:** Maggie Mouat **Copywriter:** Eugene Huane **Account Supervisors:** Nicola Harvey, Dionne Steven **Photographer:** Andrei Jewell

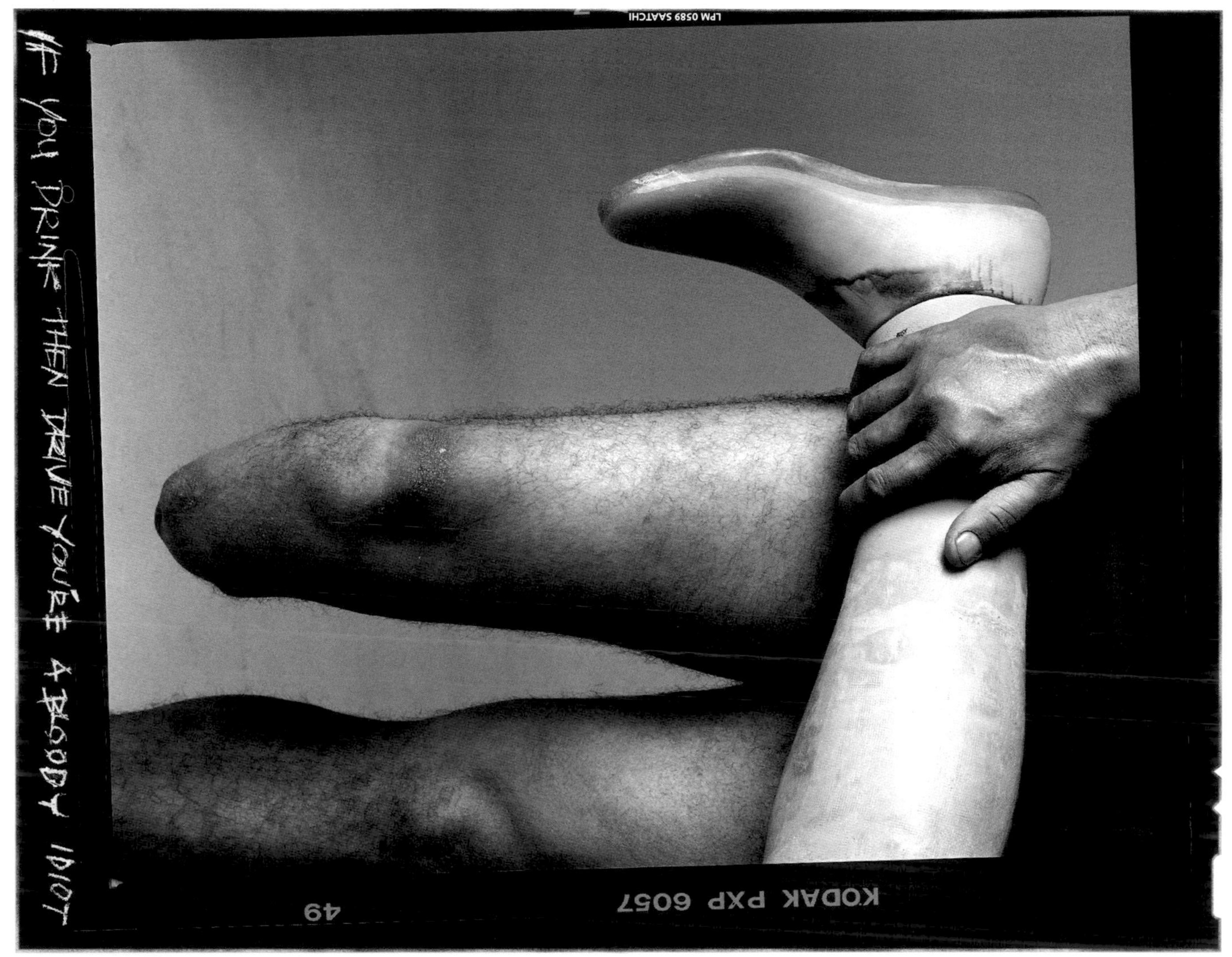

IF YOU DRINK THEN DRIVE YOU'RE A BLOODY IDIOT
LPM 0587 SAATCHI
KODAK PXP 6057

Client: Lion Breweries **Creative Director:** John McCabe **Art Director and Copywriter:** Andrew Tinning **Account Supervisor:** Derek Lockwood **Photographer:** John McDermott

Page 142 *New Zealand Symphony Orchestra* This poster accompanies a series of television and cinema commercials that demonstrate the powerful emotional effect that music played by New Zealand Symphony Orchestra has on listeners. The typography evokes musical notation and reminds the audience that hearing the NZSO is an awesome experience.

Page 143 *Auckland Regional Council* Auckland as a city gets bagged by the rest of the country as having nothing to show for itself other than traffic jams, a power crisis and yuppies. The reality is that we are surrounded by some of the world's most beautiful regional parks. Our job was to bring this alive in the minds of the popuilation. We needed more than just ads. The parks will be with us forever, and in my mind so should the communication. The parks are "natural masterpieces"—works of living art that we framed, as artists have done with their works for countless centuries. The 25 frames are permanent fixtures that will be with us for a long time to come.

Page 144-145 *Lion Breweries* While Steinlager is an incredibly popular beer with a sharp taste, it also has a reutation of having a bit of a bite the morning after. This campaign celebrates both these attributes with an underlying theme that suggests that with pleasure sometimes comes a little pain.

Page 146-147 *New Zealand Red Cross* This campaign was designed to increase Red Cross's visibility as a prelude to approaching corporates about sponsorship. As Red Cross is one of the best-known brands in the world, awareness was hardly the problem. There was, however, limited knowledge of Red Cross's proprietary right to their own emblem. In the time-honoured manner of corporate campaigns, we seizedd upon those bits of information that best illuminated the work of Red Cross and tried to express them in a compelling way. The art director had been struck by the vivid but beautiful images seen in a book on graffiti memorials in Black and Chicano communities in the US and his suggestion was to use this as an approach to the illustration. After combing Wellington for suitable demolition sites, our art director and illustrator planned each illustration for an appropriate wall.

Page 148 (left) *New Zealand Children & Young Persons Service* The brief that prompted this ad required us to raise awareness of the dangers of verbal abuse. Verbal abuse lowers the self esteem of children and creates an ongoing problem because they're likely to raise their own kids the way they were brought up. The brief asked us to make the public aware of this cycle. We wanted to create a "stop you in your tracks" ad. We were very keen to make it visually compelling. This visual was the most effective in demonstrating the endless cycle that verbal abuse can create. This ad was one component in a greater campaign that was very successful in raising awareness of the cyclical nature and consequences of verbal abuse. (right) *Stroke Foundation* This full page newspaper ad was part of a small campaign to raise awareness of the incidence of stroke in New Zealand, and to raise money for the Stroke Foundation. With very limited resources at our diposal, we wanted to make as much impact as possible. With this graphic ad, we did just that.

Page 149 (left) *AIDS Foundation of New Zealand* The idea came from a general reminder brief i.e. always use a condom. We chose this direction because the advertising (warning) worked in the same way the AIDS virus does—it's spread from person to person. We typed it, photocopied it, put a 40¢ postage stamp on the envelpe and posted it. The AIDS Foundation received a number of the letters back, which was great—it meant people were posting them on. It's still out there somewhere. (right) *State of the World Forum* This ad was part of Saatchi's global involvement in the State of the World Forum, held 31 October to 1 November 1998 in San Francisco. In addressing the problem of the global nuclear arsenal, it seemed to us hugely ironic that weapons of mass destruction were such a team effort. Our in-house illustrator drew up the mock blueprint of the bomb, which was then processed through an architect's blueprint machine—an old-fashioned and very smelly way of producing large scale accurate reproductions of plans.

Page 150-151 *Land Transport Safety Authority* We've spent a number of years showing the consequences of drunk driving. Mostly, however, we've focused on the crash itself and not the years that follow. For all of the victims featured in this campaign, the blood has dried and their scars have healed. The road to recovery ends here. For them, this is as good as it will ever get.

Page 152 *Lion Breweries* Speight's and Speight's drinkers are renown for their down to earth, no bullshit approach to life. To take the piss out of all the hoopla surrounding the millennium while every other brand and his dog were clambering for a place on the bandwagon seemed the perfect thing to do. "The Official Beer of the Old Millennium" was the stance we adopted in the months leading up to the big non-event.

Page 153 *Toyota New Zealand* Everywhere's a road with Land Cruiser. Just point your car and drive.

123-125 The Strand, Parnell P.O.Box 801 Auckland, New Zealand tel. +64-9-355-5000 fax. +64-9-379-6149
101-103 Courtenay Place P.O.Box 6540 Wellinton, New Zealand tel. +64-4-385-6524 fax. 64-4-385-9678

TBWAHuntLascaris

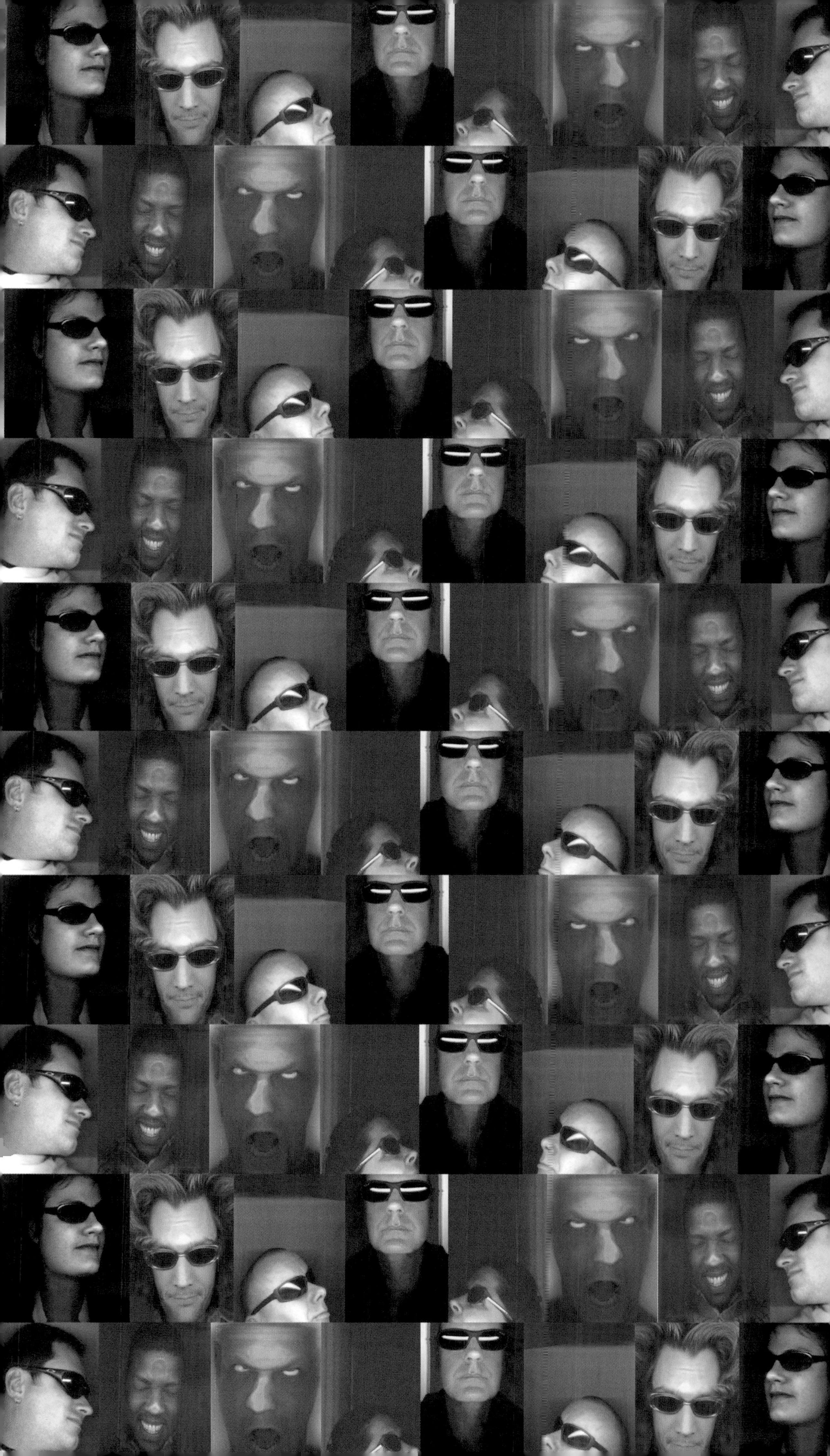

TBWAHuntLascaris

We began life as Hunt Lascaris in 1983, with the single-minded vision to be the first World Class Agency out of Africa. We started with no clients and no office. Our first campaign was sold from the back of a car. I guess you could say we were the world's first mobile agency. ■ After a year or so we found premises we could afford and became even more determined to define our agency by the quality of the work it created. (At that time it was a pretty novel approach.) Very soon our mantra became "Life's too short to be mediocre." ■ This philosophy was based on a simple observation that if you stay middle of road, you get run over both ways. Mediocre work always leaves you and your client with a sense of what might have been. I've always thought mediocrity is what slowly kills the spirit of an agency, because in a way, it's more justifiable than truly lousy work. So before you know it, Average has become your benchmark. ■ I think you can get over-academic about how great advertising or design works. In truth, it's no more complex than making a complicated thing simple and then that simple thing interesting. ■ To put it another way, your work should always be relevant but unexpectedly so. Relevance will ensure it's on strategy. The unexpected part will ensure the consumer takes the time to notice. This unexpectedness also helps you build icon brands because you have to break the rules of the category. Personally, I've always found the status quo a miserable motivator for new ideas. ■ As they say, sometimes you have to rock the boat, that's how you dislodge it from the sandbar. ■ It seems to have worked for us. In 1987 we became affiliated with TBWA. This allowed us to put exotic offices on the bottom of our letterhead and play more on a world stage. We now do a number of international assignments and the simple philosophy above seems to easily translate itself globally. ■ People comment that we have a kind of naïve courage; we happily stroll where angels fear to tread. That's fine by us, because life's an adventure of the mind. We shouldn't be scared to go where we've never been before.

Pictured left to right: Sandra de Witt, Frances Luckin, Erik Vervroegen, Tony Granger, John Hunt, Wendy Moorcroft, Jan Jacobs, T[illegible]o Mokgalagadi, Chris Garbutt and Sue Anderson

Client: Meadowfeed **Creative Director:** Sandra de Witt, Sue Anderson **Art Director:** Jamie Mietz **Copywriter:** Magriet Kruger **Photographer:** Martyn Taylor **Typographer:** Keitlwe Mametse

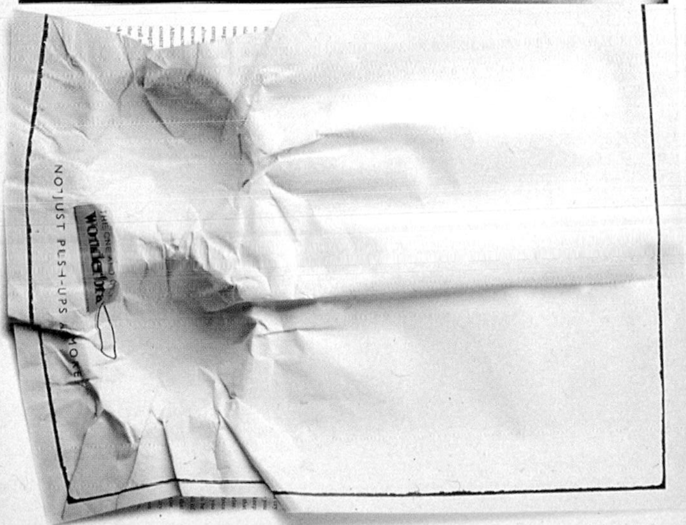

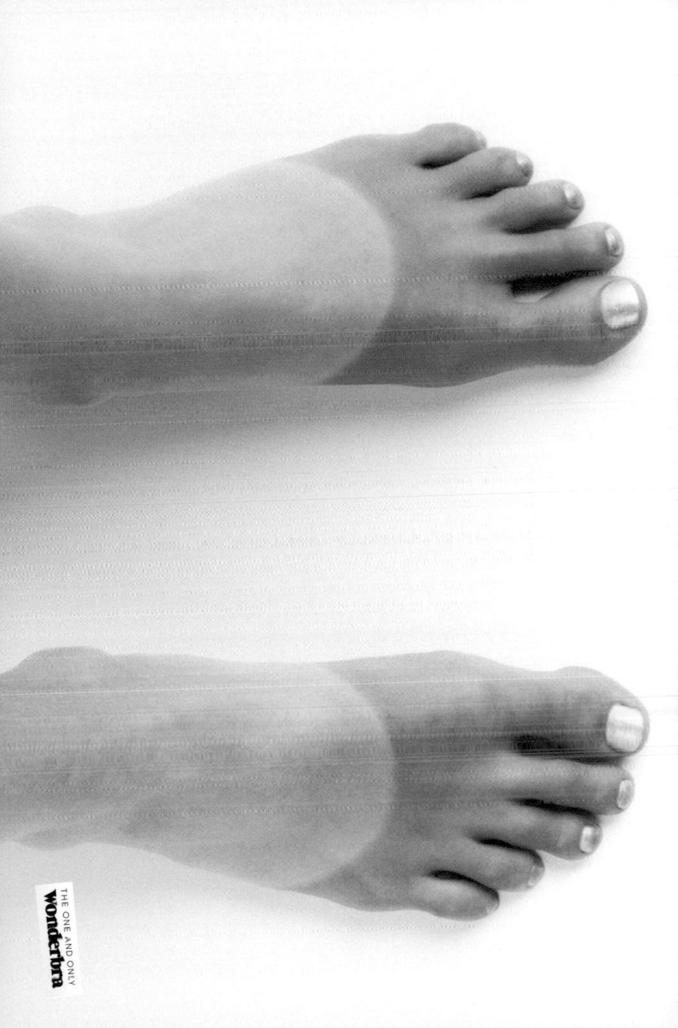

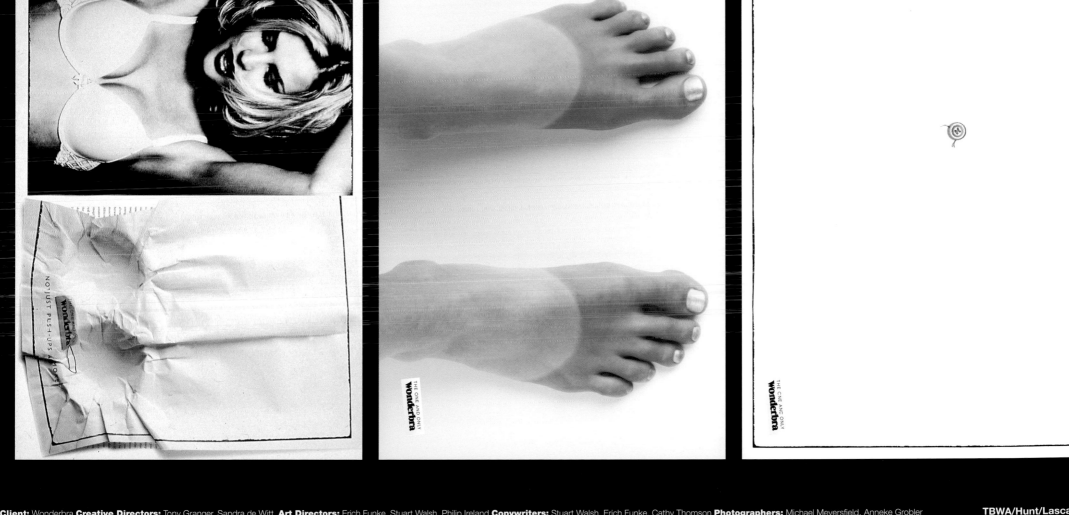

Client: Wonderbra **Creative Directors:** Tony Granger, Sandra de Witt **Art Directors:** Erich Funke, Stuart Walsh, Philip Ireland **Copywriters:** Stuart Walsh, Erich Funke, Cathy Thomson **Photographers:** Michael Meyersfield, Anneke Grobler

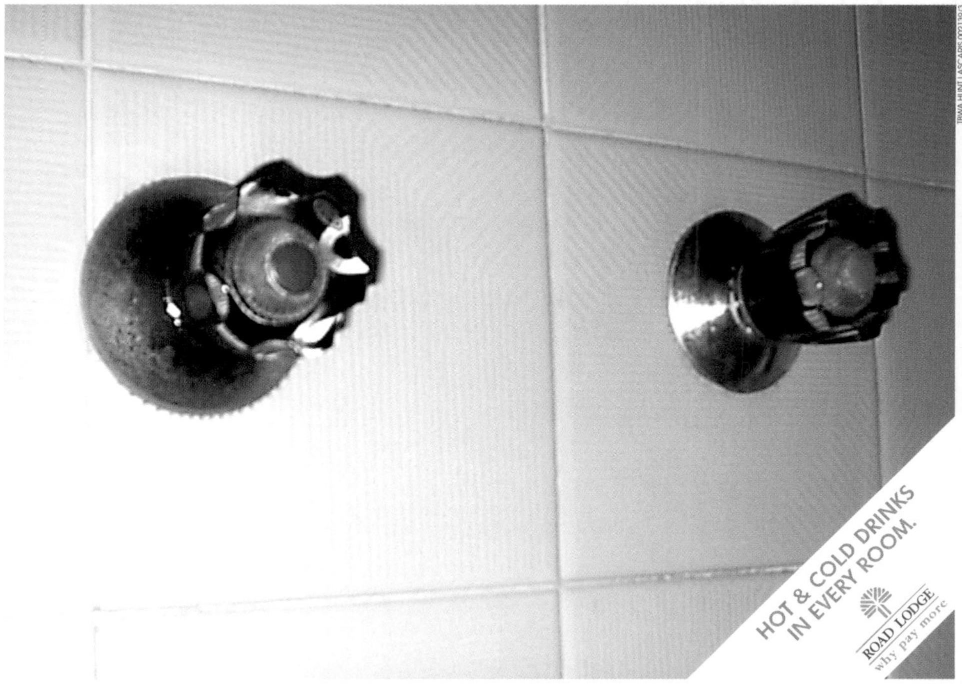

HOT & COLD DRINKS
IN EVERY ROOM.
ROAD LODGE
why pay more

TBWA HUNT LASCARIS 002139/4
HIS & HERS TOILET
FACILITIES.
ROAD LODGE
why pay more

TBWA HUNT LASCARIS 002139/2
ALL ROOMS HAVE
THEIR OWN MINI BAR.
ROAD LODGE
why pay more

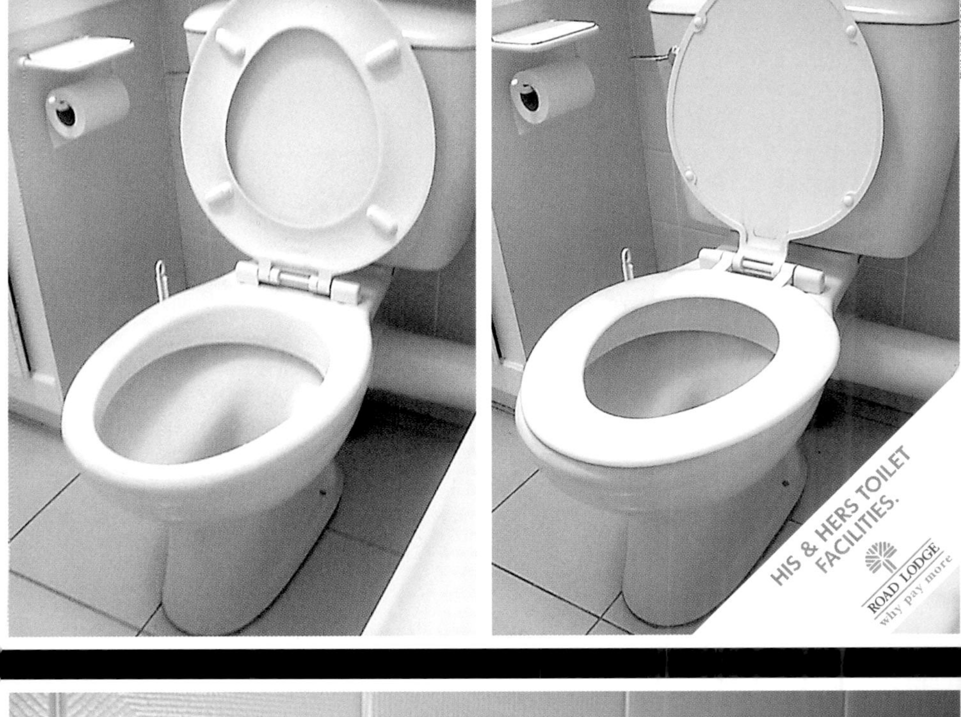

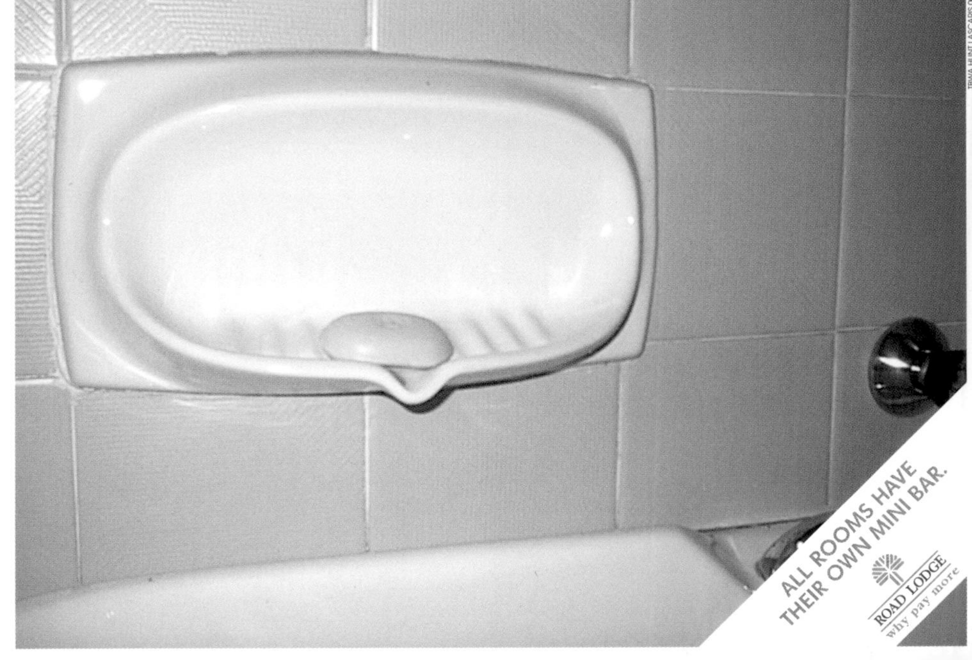

Dear Dr Andrews

I'm writing to tell you my <u>problem</u>. It seems my husband has suddenly become a sex maniac.

He makes love to me regardless of what I'm doing; ironing, washing dishes, sweeping, cooking.

I would like to know if there is anything you [illegible]

[illegible]

IT NEVER LETS YOU DOWN!

CONTAINS 700 mg GINSENG

PLUS VITAMINS

HIGH RISE

POTENT STRENGTH GINSENG CAPSULES

LAND ROVER
DEFENDER. THE ORIGINAL 4x4.
LAND ROVER
GAME VIEWER
LAND ROVER
DEFENDER. DIE OORSPRONKLIKE 4x4.

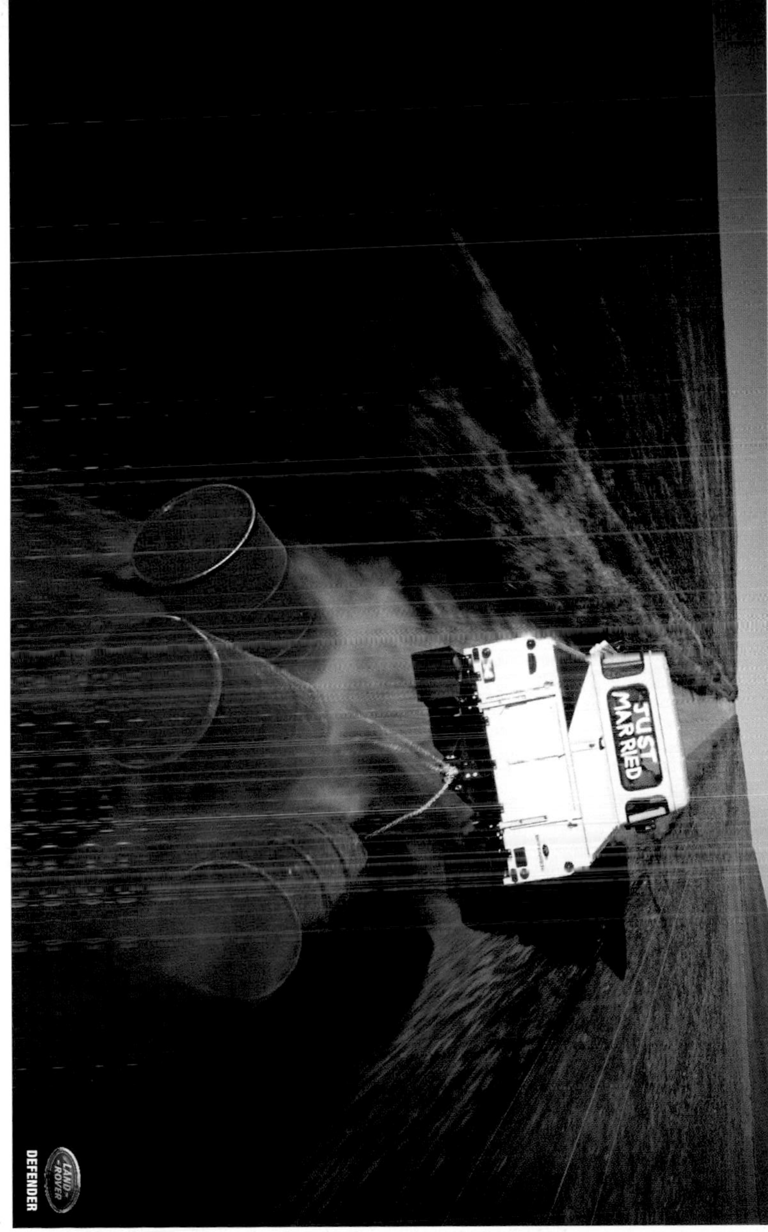

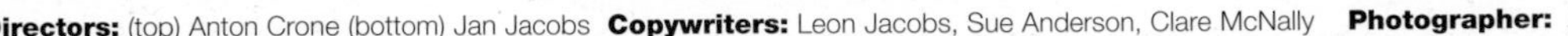

Client: Land Rover **Creative Directors:** (top) Sandra de Witt, Sue Anderson (bottom) Tony Granger **Art Directors:** (top) Anton Crone (bottom) Jan Jacobs **Copywriters:** Leon Jacobs, Sue Anderson, Clare McNally **Photographer:** Martyn Taylor

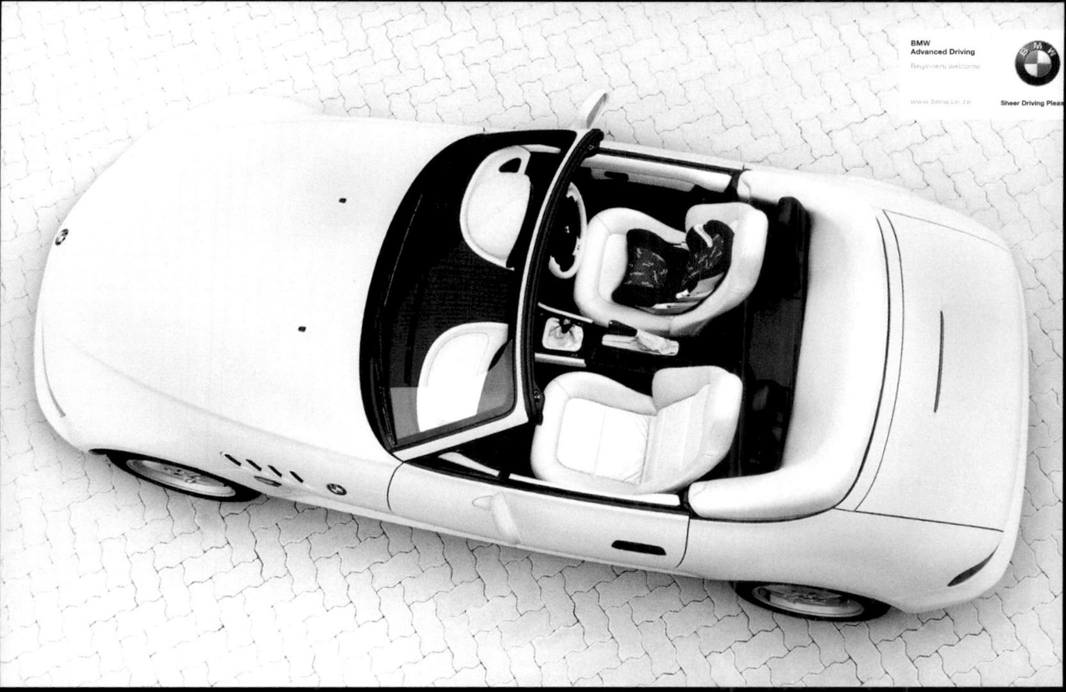

BMW
Advanced Driving
Beginners welcome
www.bmw.co.za
Sheer Driving Pleas

The new, more powerful BMW 320d
www.bmw.co.za
Sheer Driving Pleasure

The new 3 Series Convertible
0-100 : 7.4 sec
300 Nm @ 3 500rpm
170 kW
www.bmw.co.za
Sheer Driving Pleasure

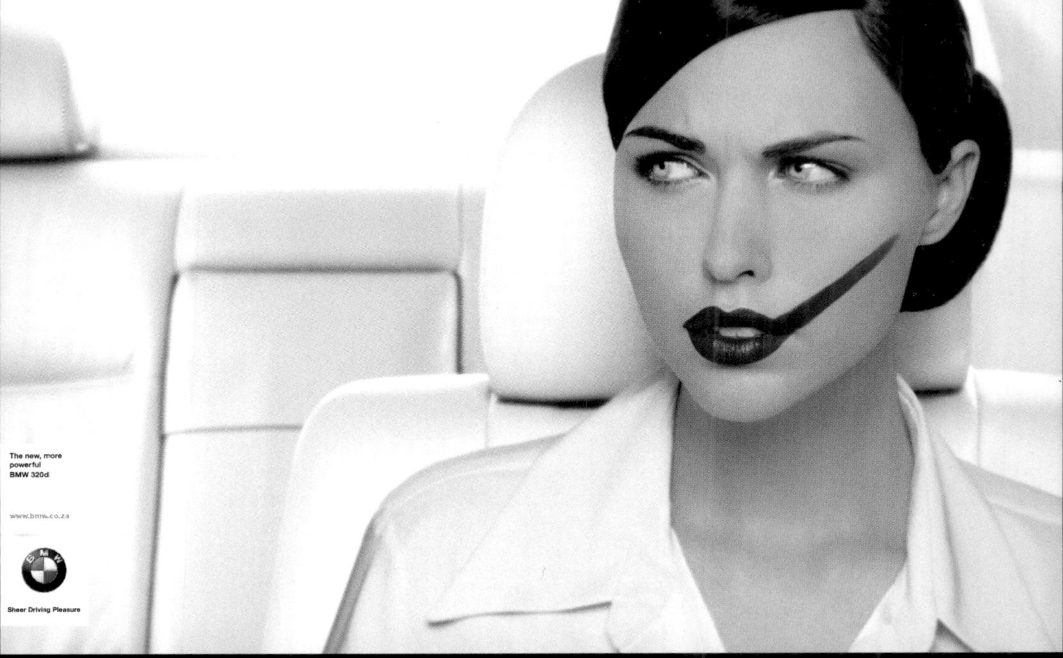

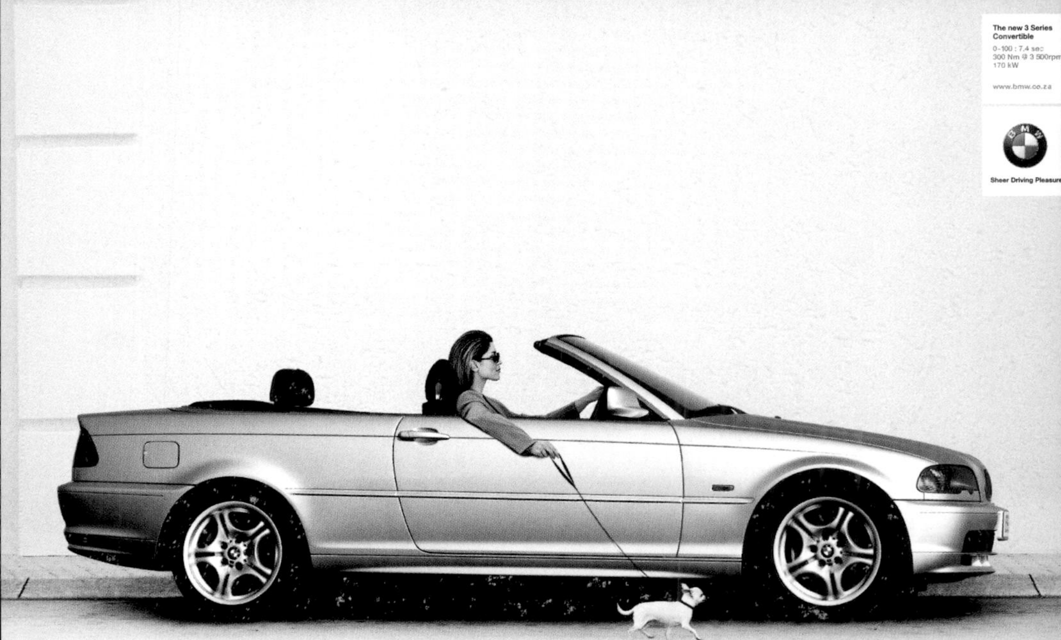

*Initially available in Pretoria East, Sandton, Randburg, Randburg North, Midrand, Centurion and Waterval.

BMW
Satellite Navigation
Available in
all sedan models

www.bmw.co.za

BMW

Sheer Driving Pleasure

Now you can drive a car so intelligent, you'll never get lost. After pioneering Satellite Navigation for the world BMW is the first to introduce it in South Africa*. To make arriving at your destination considerably easier.

SELECT

START

BMW

Sheer Driving Pleasure.

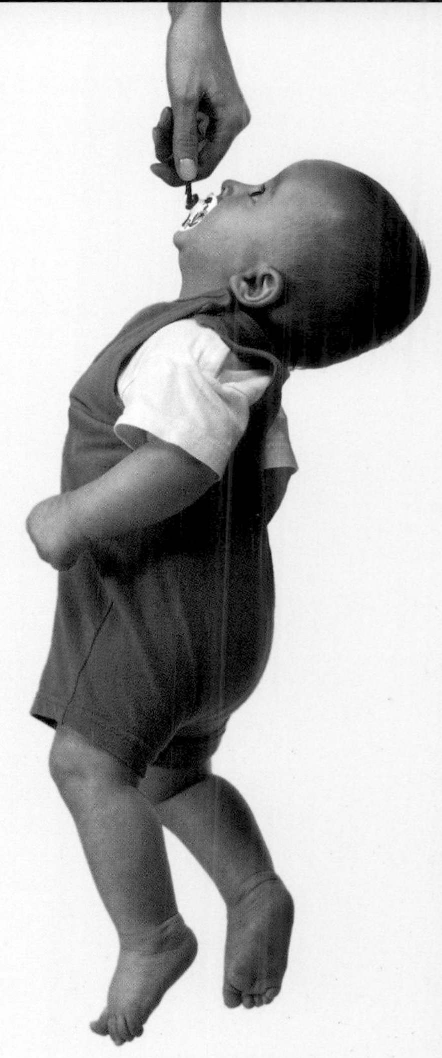

For healthy teeth and a correct bite, 8 out of 10 orthodontists* recommend Nuk before any other brand.

NUK®

UK **Creative Directors:** Tony Granger, Erich Funke **Art Directors:** Gareth Lessing, Colin Jeffrey **Copywriter:** Marike Venter **Photographer:** Michael Lewis

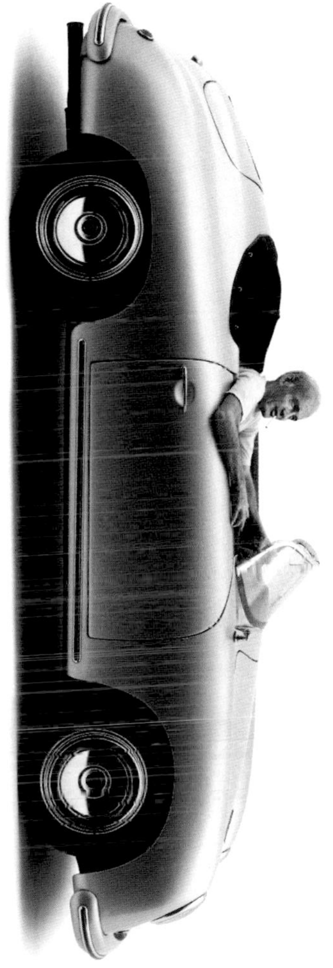

Client: (top) The Spy Shop (middle) BMW (bottom) Dunlop **Creative Director:** Tony Granger **Art Directors:** Jan Jacobs, Lapeace Kakaza, Erik Vervroegen **Copywriters:** Clare McNally, Mitchell Alison, Porky Hefer

Heritage
Bakery
wicked fruit cake

Client: BIC **Creative Director:** Tony Granger **Art Director:** Jan Jacobs **Copywriter:** Clare McNally **Photographer:** David Prior **Illustrator:** Jan Jacobs

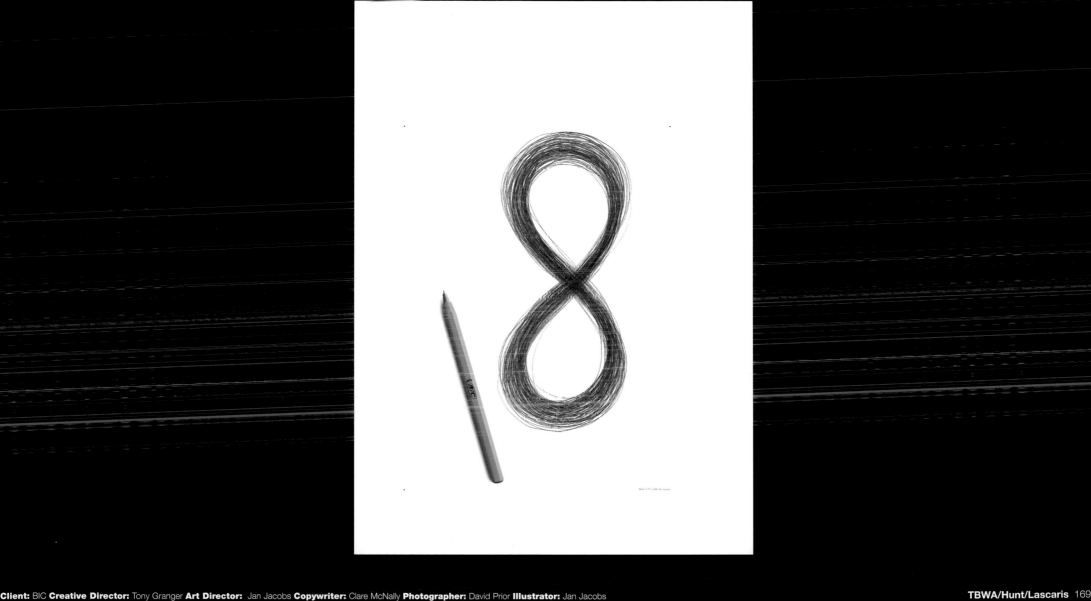

Page 158 *Meadowfeed* This category is over-burdened with technical information and livestock staring mournfully at the reader. We were asked to succinctly display the health-giving qualities of Meadowfeed, which promises "better performing cows".

Page 159 *Wonderbra* The benefits of wearing a Wonderbra are pretty obvious and self-explanatory. Instead of just stating the obvious, the trick was to engage the reader in a humorous way.

Page 160 *Road Lodge* Road Lodge is a budget hotel, but a proud and very successful budget hotel. Their self-confidence is evident in the fact that they can laugh at themselves. (These ads were also used as leaflets placed in the back pockets of economy class airline seats.)

Page 161 *High Rise* Before there was Viagra, there was Ginseng backed High Rise. Hubba! Hubba!

Page 162 *Land Rover* In Africa, Land Rover is an icon brand. It's less of a vehicle and more an indelible part of the landscape. While other brands claim a tough 4 x 4 image, only Land Rover is "Africa tested." It is steeped in the red sand and rolling savannah of this tough continent.

Page 163 *Land Rover* (top) The Range Rover sits at the very top of the social gene pool. It's the new Millenium status symbol. Even similar icons of the past acknowledge this. (bottom) The Defender is seen by the farming community as the ultimate work horse. It also has incredible towing capabilities.

Page 164 *BMW* (top) BMW not only makes a magnificent motor vehicle, it also happily teaches you how to drive it. If you're humbled when you first sit behind the wheel, you'll soon grow into the full understanding of "Sheer Driving Pleasure". (middle) The BMW 320d has a lot going for it, but the most immediately compelling is its incredible acceleration. (bottom) The BMW Convertible is so magnificently ergonomically designed, when you're outdoors you'll find any excuse to stay behind the wheel.

Page 165 *BMW* (top) Fulfilling the promise of always being on the edge of technical innovation, BMW's Satellite Navigation system almost literally gives the driver another pair of eyes. (bottom) When the control panel moved to the steering wheel, Sheer Driving Pleasure was just a fingertip away.

Page 166 *NUK* NUK products are all orthodontically designed and perfectly nipple shaped. Who'd want to let go?

Page 167 (top) *The Spy Shop* It's always fun to get to the very essence of the brand. This small space ad was then translated into a Corporate Identity package. (middle) *BMW* The majority of these BMW bikers are men desperately trying to avert a mid-life crisis. They want to feel the wind through their hair again (if they still have hair). However, since they last drove a motorbike twenty years ago, a refresher course is not a bad idea. (bottom) *Dunlop* Dunlop's promise of "Tested for the Unexpected" gets the back-to-the-future treatment. James Dean would've made a cool grandfather.

Page 168 *Heritage Bakery* Lead me not into temptation. Cake that is so good it's ba-a-a-d.

Page 169 *BIC* The promise of BIC pens is simple; a utilitarian writing instrument that just keeps on keeping on.

51 Wierda Road West Wierda Valley 2196 Sandton South Africa Tel: +27-11-322-3100 Fax: +27-11-884-3818

It's hard to tear yourself away from this NUK ad by TBWA; photo by Michael Lewis (see page 166)

Graphis 328
Bianco & Cucco
Mark Hess
Heye & Partner
BlackDog®
Ravenwood
Newman
BIANCO & CUCCO / MARK HESS / HEYE & PARTNER / BLACKDOG / RAVENWOOD / NEWMAN